PASTOR AND PEOPLE

Making Mutual Ministry Work

Augsburg Fortress

Minneapolis

PASTOR AND PEOPLE
Making Mutual Ministry Work

Developed in cooperation with the Evangelical Lutheran Church in America's Division for Ministry and the Division for Congregational Ministries, Richard Bruesehoff and Michael R. Rothaar, project managers.

Scripture quotations are from *New Revised Standard Version Bible*, copyright © 1989 Division of Christian Education of the National Council of the Churches of Christ in the United States of America. Used by permission.

Editors: Laurie J. Hanson, Ivy M. Palmer

Cover design and series logo: Marti Naughton
Text design: James Satter
Cover photograph: Gordon Gray, FRPS

About the cover image: The centerpiece of the Resurrection Window in First Lisburn Presbyterian Church, Northern Ireland, was created by stained glass artist James Watson, Belfast, from fragments of church windows destroyed by a car bomb in 1981 and restored after a second bomb in 1989. The window symbolizes new life in Christ, which transforms darkness to light, hatred to love, despair to hope, and death to life. The members of First Lisburn Presbyterian have lived out this promise through new initiatives for community service, reconciliation, and peace-making.

ISBN 978-0-8066-4651-0

✠ Contents

Preface

Letter of Call to an ordained minister of the Evangelical Lutheran Church in America

We call you to exercise among us the ministry of Word and Sacrament which God has established and which the Holy Spirit empowers: to preach and teach the Word of God in accordance with the Holy Scriptures and the Lutheran Confessions; to administer Holy Baptism and Holy Communion; to lead us in worship; to proclaim the forgiveness of sins; to provide pastoral care; to speak for justice in behalf of the poor and oppressed; to encourage persons to prepare for the ministry of the Gospel; to impart knowledge of the Evangelical Lutheran Church in America and its wider ministry; to endeavor to increase support given by our congregation to the work of our whole church; to equip us for witness and service; and guide us in proclaiming God's love through word and deed.

In accepting this call, you hereby promise to fulfill this pastoral ministry in accord with the standards and policies for ordained ministers of the Evangelical Lutheran Church in America. Therefore, be diligent in the study of Holy Scripture, in use of the means of grace, in prayer, in faithful service, and in holy living.

With this call, we pledge our prayers, love, esteem, and personal support for the sake of the ministry entrusted to you by God and for our ministry together in Christ's name. Specific responsibilities, compensation, benefits, and conditions of this call are contained in a document related to this call.

Chapter 1

Tending the Garden

Richard Bruesehoff

"Pastor Rodriguez, will you love, serve and pray for God's people? Will you nourish them with the Word and Holy Sacraments, leading them by your own example in the use of the means of grace, in faithful service and holy living?"

"I will, and I ask God to help me."

"And you, people of God, will you pray for her, help and honor her for her work's sake, and in all things strive to live together in the peace and unity of Christ?"

"We will."

> *Occasional Services, A Companion to Lutheran Book of Worship,*
> Minneapolis: Augsburg and Philadelphia: Board of Publication,
> Lutheran Church in America, 1990, p. 225, 226

Have you ever planted a vegetable or flower garden? If you have, then you know that gardening is a year-round task.

Sometime during the cold, dreary months of winter the first seed catalogue will arrive in the mail. With its arrival you begin the annual process of planning for next year's garden. Which flowers will thrive

---

Richard (Dick) Bruesehoff serves as the director for leadership support in the ELCA Division for Ministry. During his previous calls as a parish pastor and assistant to the bishop, he has learned much about the importance of the relationships between pastor and people for vital, faithful ministry.

in this climate? Which ones performed well last year? Which fruits and vegetables will grace your table during the summer, fall, and winter months?

When warmer weather arrives, you gather the right tools, till the soil, plant selected seeds and seedlings, and fertilize. As the weeks progress, you do the hot, sweaty work of weeding and thinning. You pull early-bearing plants and re-seed with later-bearing varieties.

During the waning days of summer and the cooler days of fall, you enjoy the harvest. If you live in a climate where the approach of winter signals the end of the growing season, you pull the dying plants and ready the ground for its fallow time. All the while you assess the past growing season and enjoy the produce.

Any gardener who plants and expects an instant harvest without the day-to-day work of tending is going to be disappointed—and unsuccessful!

Tending a congregation

Leading and shaping the life of a congregation require no less attention and tending. Congregational leaders, like gardeners, must be constantly involved in planning, tending, and assessing. What ministries have grown in this soil in the past? Which are suited to our local growing conditions now and into the future? You'll need to ask whether you have the tools and resources you need.

This image of a cross indicates that further information on a topic appears in another book in the Congregational Leader Series.

At times a congregation may need to pull up dying ministries in order to make room for new ones. This is an opportunity to look back with gratitude at the produce of last year's garden, like the gardener at the end of the growing season. It is also an opportunity to look forward with hope to the promise of next year's garden.

You may have already discovered other volumes in the Congregational Leader Series that have proven to be good tools for tending your congregation. *Our Context* and *Our Mission* look at your congregation's mission in the community you serve. *Our Structure* can guide you in organizing the congregation. *Our Stewardship* and *Our*

Gifts help with assessing and celebrating the gifted people and abundant resources with which God has blessed your congregation. *Our Staff* is devoted to the details of building and supporting a staff team. *Our Community* is a resource for those who are working with the kinds of disagreements and conflicts that are part of the normal life of congregations.

But there's another kind of tending that always seems to be part of healthy, vital congregations. That's tending what is arguably the most critical relationship in the congregation, the relationship between pastor and people. These next pages are meant to guide you, pastor and people, as you attend to the relationships that undergird every aspect of the life and ministry of your congregation. For those of you who are called, elected, and appointed to leadership positions in your congregation, this tending just may be the most important part of your work. Any congregation that expects to maintain the working relationship between pastor and people without the day-to-day work of tending is going to be disappointed—and unsuccessful!

Your tending is essential to producing a harvest of lively, healthy ministry.

Gardens are meant to produce

While some seeds may look strange, planting instructions may be ambiguous, and the design of a cultivator may leave you baffled, the gardener's task is clear. You are tending a garden. You're not designing a house or playing a game of baseball. You're tending a garden. And gardens are meant to grow, to produce things satisfying to the taste buds and beautiful to the eye.

Practicing leadership in a congregation and understanding the relationships between pastor and people can be no less puzzling. But you know what you're doing. You're leading a congregation. You are members of the holy, catholic church, the communion of saints, the body of Christ. And your tending is essential to producing a harvest of lively, healthy ministry.

God is calling your congregation to mission, to ministry: "But you will receive power when the Holy Spirit has come upon you; and you will be my witnesses in Jerusalem, in all Judea and Samaria, and to the ends of the earth" (Acts 1:8). Every congregation shares this same call to be living witnesses—to celebrate God's power to gather alienated people, to proclaim God's love for all people, to live gratefully and joyfully, to explore together what it means to be witnesses to the world, and to serve other people as Jesus served.

The ground we plant in

God is passionate about being in a relationship with us.

So you're a congregation with a mission. It's God's mission that shapes the day-to-day lives of people. But just exactly who are we talking about? And how is God getting this mission accomplished? Our own theological tradition has always been good soil in which to grow ministry.

We begin with a clear understanding that God wants nothing more than to have a relationship with us. What could make it clearer than Jesus' own words?: "For God so loved the world that he gave his only Son, so that everyone who believes in him may not perish but may have eternal life. Indeed, God did not send the Son into the world to condemn the world, but in order that the world might be saved through him" (John 3:16-17). God desires nothing more than to be your God, my God, our God. God is passionate about being in a relationship with us. For many, that relationship begins with baptism.

But God has gone even farther. God hasn't left us guessing about the purpose or intention of this relationship. God became one of us in Jesus Christ, a child born into a human family, as the living witness to God's intention. God wants us to know, to live with the certainty, that God loves us. God loves you. God loves me. Listen to Jesus' preaching and teaching. Watch him in action. There can be no doubt.

But there's even more to the picture than this relationship of love, renewed every day. As Martin Luther instructed families in his Small Catechism (*The Book of Concord: The Confessions of the Evangelical Lutheran Church*, Robert Kolb and Timothy J. Wengert, ed., Minneapolis: Fortress Press, 2000):

In the morning, as soon as you get out of bed, you are to make the sign of the holy cross and say:

"God the Father, Son, and Holy Spirit watch over me. Amen"

Then, kneeling or standing, say the Apostles' Creed and the Lord's Prayer. If you wish, you may in addition recite this little prayer as well:

"I give thanks to you, my heavenly Father through Jesus Christ your dear Son, that you have protected me this night from all harm and danger, and I ask you that you would also protect me today from sin and all evil, so that my life and actions may please you completely. For into your hands I commend myself: my body, my soul, and all that is mine. Let your holy angel be with me, so that the wicked foe may have no power over me. Amen"

After singing a hymn perhaps . . . or whatever else may serve your devotion, *you are to go to your work joyfully* (p. 363, italics added).

Baptism is not only the beginning of our relationship with God, it is also the beginning of our life's work, our calling, our ministry. Lutherans call this the priesthood of all believers. In this relationship we understand that our work, our vocation, is not only the way we make a living. It is the way in which we live our baptismal relationships with God, all of creation, and every human being. God prepares us for our vocation by giving each of us gifts essential to the community's common, shared work of gathering, praising, teaching, proclaiming, and serving. Chapter 2 takes us deeper into this understanding of baptism as our common call to ministry.

God prepares us for our life's work, our vocation.

We are not left alone to discover our gifts for ministry and respond to our life's calling. It's in the strong, healthy relationships between all who are baptized and the pastors whom they have called to lead them that we discover and explore the gifts given to each of us. In the relationships between pastor and people we participate in the renewal of our own baptismal promises (*Lutheran Book of Worship*, Minneapolis: Augsburg and Philadelphia, Board of Publication, Lutheran Church in America, 1978):

> You have made public profession of your faith. Do you intend to continue in the covenant God made with you in Holy Baptism:
>
> to live among God's faithful people,
>
> to hear his Word and share in his supper,
>
> to proclaim the good news of God in Christ through word and deed,
>
> to serve all people, following the example of our Lord Jesus, and to strive for justice and peace in all the earth?

And we respond, 'I do, and I ask God to help and guide me' (p. 201).

"And I ask God to help and guide me"

Do you have the courage simply to say "yes" to those questions? Would you dare to pledge your entire life to God's love, justice, and peace in every word and action?

Christians live with an understanding that God has not left us alone to figure this out and put it into action all by ourselves. In fact we confess regularly that, left to ourselves, we couldn't and wouldn't figure it out (*With One Voice*, Minneapolis: Augsburg Fortress, 1995): "We confess that we are in bondage to sin and cannot free ourselves. We have sinned against you in thought, word, and deed, by what we have done and by what we have left undone" (p. 11). As our whole relationship with God begins with Jesus Christ, so does our ability to carry out these promises. The Augsburg Confession, a core declaration of faith for Lutherans, puts it this way:

> [We] teach that human beings cannot be justified before God by their own powers, merits, or works. But they are justified as a gift on account of Christ through faith when we believe that Christ has suffered for us and that for his sake our sin is forgiven and righteousness and eternal life are given to us. For God will regard and reckon this faith as righteousness in his sight, as St. Paul says in Romans 3 and 4 (*The Book of Concord*, pp. 39-40).

God really is passionate about this relationship with us, a relationship in which we come to understand both our life's work and God's love for us. Understanding the relationship and our life's work can't and won't happen by itself. God uses the teaching of the Gospel and the sacraments of Baptism and Holy Communion to draw us into the relationship and show us our life's work. And God also uses people, pastors in particular, to proclaim the Gospel to us and administer the sacraments for us:

> So that we may obtain this faith, the ministry of teaching the gospel and administering the sacraments was instituted. For through the Word and the sacraments as through instruments the Holy Spirit is given, who effects faith where and when it pleases God in those who hear the gospel, that is to say, in those who hear that God, not on account of our own merits but on account of Christ, justifies those who believe that they are received into grace on account of Christ (The Augsburg Confession, *The Book of Concord*, p. 41).

Pastors are called to the task of becoming tools in God's hands. They are called to help us confidently say "yes" to God's call to "proclaim the good news of God in Christ through word and deed, to serve all people, following the example of our Lord Jesus, and to strive for justice and peace in all the earth" (*Lutheran Book of Worship*, p. 201). Pastors are part of what helps and guides us when we say, "and I ask God to help and guide me." It is pastors who are charged with leading us in ministry. It is pastors who are called to preach, teach, care for us, and lead us in ways that make God's love for us crystal clear and prepare us for our ministries, our life's work.

Pastors are called to and charged with the task of becoming tools in God's hands.

Tending the changing relationships

In most congregations, and throughout much of American society, the image and role of pastor—and the relationship between pastor and people—has undergone enormous change. As recently as 50 years ago, pastors were often among the most highly educated people in a community. Some congregations still act as if that were the case. In

There will be much in this book that also applies to the relationships between congregations and other staff members including associates in ministry; diaconal ministers; deaconesses; and those who lead ministries of music, education, health, or youth. But *Pastor and People: Making Mutual Ministry Work* will keep its focus specifically on the unique relationship between pastor and people.

these congregations the pastor is expected to be at the center of every decision and every action. Congregations like these begin to assume that their role is simply to support the ministry of the pastor with their money and perhaps with their prayers. And even if members of the congregation no longer believe it, and would never allow anyone else such unilateral authority, they act as if the church really is mostly about the pastor.

In some congregations the relationship between pastor and people has become more like that of employee and employer or provider and consumer. Pastors are expected to do ministry to and for people, who become the passive consumers of a congregation's ministry. This view of the relationship between pastor and people jeopardizes the understanding that we are all called to ministry by our baptism. If we hold this view, we risk losing our identity as people to whom God has generously and lovingly given gifts. We risk giving up our role as people God is using to love all of creation back to life.

Other recent events have led to a general suspicion toward those in any position of leadership and to the erosion of the authority of the pastoral office. Scandals involving church leaders, including financial and sexual misconduct and other abuses of power, have chipped away at many people's confidence in pastors.

Congregations in which lack of confidence in pastors is the prevailing attitude might act as if they don't want or need a pastor. Congregations like these risk losing the confidence that God has called pastors to lead us, challenge us, call us forward, and keep us equipped for our ministries. They risk refusing one of God's gifts—pastors who are prepared and called to lead us in ministry.

The stole that a pastor wears is the visible symbol of a very different kind of relationship. The stole symbolizes the leadership of service described in the *Model Constitution for Congregations of the Evangelical Lutheran Church in America* (Evangelical Lutheran Church in America, 2001, C9.03):

Every ordained minister shall:

preach the Word;

administer the sacraments;

conduct public worship;

provide pastoral care; and

speak publicly to the world in solidarity with the poor and

oppressed, calling for justice and proclaiming God's love

for the world.

Each ordained minister with a congregational call shall, within the con-

gregation:

offer instruction, confirm, marry, visit the sick and distressed, and bury

the dead;

supervise all schools and organizations of this congregation;

install regularly elected members of the Congregation Council;

and with the council, administer discipline.

Every pastor shall:

strive to extend the Kingdom of God in the community, in the nation,

and abroad;

seek out and encourage qualified persons to prepare for the ministry of

the Gospel;

impart knowledge of this church and its wider ministry through distri-

bution of its periodicals and other publications; and endeavor to

increase the support given by the congregation to the work of the

churchwide organization of the Evangelical Lutheran Church in

America and of the synod (p. 13).

This is the ministry to which pastors are called. This is the authority entrusted to pastors, to lead like a shepherd, not a hired hand. And it's the beginning of the relationship between pastor and

The stole that a pastor wears symbolizes the leadership of service.

people. You'll read much more about the pastor's role in this relationship in Chapter 3.

As the roles and expectations of pastors continue to change, the relationships between pastor and people require tending. And tending the relationships between all those who are baptized and the pastors they have called to lead them will help us clarify and reclaim the public office of pastor and allow us to grow more deeply into our own ministries.

Constant tending

By now, you've heard enough about the relationships—between God and humankind, between church and world, between pastor and people—to know that our ministries don't happen by accident. And they don't happen in isolation. They are discovered, explored, and supported in the relationships that exist within the whole church and in every congregation. But when these relationships are neglected, the ministry of the whole church is likely to suffer.

The Apostle Paul wrote a letter to the church in Philippi from his prison cell. Paul, who had spent time with the congregation, wrote, "I thank my God every time I remember you, constantly praying with joy in every one of my prayers for all of you, because of your sharing in the gospel from the first day until now" (Philippians 1:3-5). But because he apparently had gotten wind that relationships between himself and some within the congregation had become strained in his absence, he wrote further, "Therefore, my beloved, just as you have always obeyed me, not only in my presence, but much more now in my absence, work out your own salvation with fear and trembling; for it is God who is at work in you, enabling you both to will and to work for his good pleasure" (Philippians 2:12-13). In *Philippians, Interpretation: A Bible Commentary for Teaching* (Atlanta: John Knox Press, 1985), Fred B. Craddock comments on Paul's letter:

> We can understand, then, that if some in Philippi felt they were not
> within Paul's love, the loss was not just personal but ecclesiological,

ethical and soteriological. We can understand, also, that if their relationship were predicated entirely upon his presence or entirely upon his absence rather than upon a partnership, a fellowship, a participation that survived both intimacy and distance, then it is not just friendship that is lost but their life together "in Christ Jesus" (p. 45).

Paul seems to have recognized that the challenges facing a congregation do not stand still and the opportunities and needs for ministry are constantly changing. We also see that in Philippi, as in any other congregation, the health of the relationships between the pastor and the congregation has an impact on how the congregation responds to those challenges, opportunities, and needs. For this reason, the relationships must constantly be tended.

Tending the relationship between pastor and people is hard, sweaty, necessary work to which every congregation must give attention. Tending the relationship between pastor and people is part of the prayerful work that every congregation must do as it explores ever more deeply what it means to live faithfully in relationship to God and each other. Tending the relationship between pastor and people, the relationship from which a congregation's ministries flow, is crucial work for congregational leaders.

Chapter 4 explores the concept that stands behind this book, truly mutual ministry. *The Model Constitution* (chapter 13, p. 20) requires the establishment of only five committees: executive, nominating, audit, call, and mutual ministry. However, since its inception, there has been confusion about the role of the mutual ministry committee and its place within the organizational and organic composition of the congregation. Central to an understanding of the mutual ministry committee's tasks, however, are a broad vision of ministry and a healthy practice of mutuality.

Organic and organizational

Like tending a garden, tending the relationship between pastor and people takes a number of different forms. Attention must be given to the less straightforward, more organic tending of the relationship

Tending the relationship between pastor and people is crucial work for congregational leaders.

between pastor and people. This is attention given to the ebb and flow of human relationships. It's the tending that takes into account the unique character (might we even say characters?) of those who populate the pews and the pulpits, who preside at the altars and who pass in and out of the doors of your church.

Chapter 5 focuses on support for pastoral ministry and explores the unique dual role of the pastor who, like every member, is one of the baptized, yet by training, ordination, and call is set apart for a specific ministry. This creates a challenge for the pastor to find places where he or she can be physically, spiritually, and personally renewed. Some support can and must come from within the congregation. But some can only come from outside, from people who are not connected with the life of the congregation.

Some of the tending of the relationship between pastor and people is straightforward organizational, administrative work. It is the work of a call committee, charged with the responsibility to lead the search for a pastor and begin the new relationship between pastor and people. It is the work of a ministry review team. If, as we believe, the purpose of a congregation is to give witness to God in the world and to equip every person for ministry, someone has to ask regularly, "How are we doing?" Chapter 6 outlines a process for establishing goals and direction for your congregation. These goals and direction become the basis for annual ministry review and performance evaluation, of both the congregation's ministry and the pastor's ministry.

The organizational, administrative tending of the relationship is also the work of the personnel committee, charged with tending the environment in which pastor and people work together. Chapter 7 offers very practical guidance and tools to those who are responsible for tending this aspect of the relationship between pastor and people.

Many people share the responsibility for tending the relationship between pastor and people.

Those who tend the relationship

Many people share the responsibility for tending the relationship between pastor and people. We believe that God calls people to be pastors and the whole church affirms that when a pastor is ordained. We also believe that the people of a particular congregation call a particular person to be their pastor. The whole church affirms that when a pastor is installed.

Pastors who are serving congregations certainly have a role in tending the relationship between pastor and people. In addition, an interim pastor serving a congregation during a time of transition has a unique opportunity for tending this relationship. The growing number of those who are serving congregations in synodically authorized ministries also must give attention to the relationship between pastor and people.

Many laypersons may be responsible for tending the relationship between pastor and people. The individuals and groups with this responsibility vary from one setting to another, depending on the congregation's structure and size. The call committee will have the work of tending the relationship during a pastoral transition. In most congregations this tending will be part of the work of the congregation council. It will also be part of the work of other congregational groups such as a mutual ministry committee, pastor/parish relations committee, staff support committee, personnel committee, or finance committee. In your congregation there may be other groups that are authorized to attend to the relationship between pastor and people.

Others become tenders of the relationship from time to time. During times of pastoral transition, conflict, or congregational transition, the synod bishop or a member of the bishop's staff may become involved in the relationship between pastor and people. Those called upon to be congregational resource people and consultants also may play this role.

Tools for the tenders

Every congregation is called to a common mission—to be a living witness to God in the world. Every pastor is called to a common set of responsibilities and tasks associated with the pastoral office. But the particular kind of tending required for your particular congregation is likely to be different from what is required in another congregation. The relationship between pastor and people, and the kind of tending that it requires, may not be the same in small and large congregations; in rural, urban, and suburban areas; or in communities that are growing and those where the population is declining. The task of tending the relationship between pastor and people will need to reflect the unique history and ethnic composition of your community.

The chapters that follow and the tools associated with each probably won't work as one-size-fits-all tools. They'll work better as part of a large, well-equipped toolbox. The advantage of having a well-equipped toolbox—and knowing how to use each of the tools—is that this enables you to adapt to the unique circumstances of your own congregation.

Pastor and people

While only some are called to be pastors, everyone is called to ministry. One of the signs of God's reforming, renewing power must cer-

Although the functions of mutual ministry, evaluation, and personnel are explored in separate chapters in this book, the vast majority of ELCA congregations don't have the large pool of people required to create separate discrete groups for each of these. As you read, note which groups in your congregation are carrying out the functions of mutual ministry, evaluation, and personnel. If there is no personnel committee in your congregation, the finance committee or congregation council may turn to the executive committee or others when budgeting for the pastor's compensation. If there is no mutual ministry committee, the *Model Constitution* requires that the executive committee assume this function (C13.04).

No matter how your congregation is structured to handle mutual ministry, evaluation, and personnel, the issues are entirely separate and should be handled separately. If one group (such as the executive committee) assumes all three functions, it will need to clearly delineate the times when it is dealing with mutual ministry, evaluation, or personnel.

> The reproducible tools in this book can be downloaded and customized at www.augsburgfortress.org/CLS.

tainly be a growing celebration of the understanding that ministry is the proper, common calling of all the baptized. Everyone, including pastors—perhaps especially pastors—can celebrate our shared baptismal ministry.

The Evangelical Lutheran Church in America (ELCA) ordains and authorizes pastors for the work of publicly leading congregations in ministry. Congregations call and authorize pastors from this roster for the work of ministry with them. The church throughout the world and through the ages has given pastors the authority to preach and preside and to serve as one who calls us, challenges us, and prepares us for our ministries. This work of ministry, both our common baptismal ministry and the specific ministry of pastors, is most faithful and effective when the relationship between pastor and people is well tended.

For discussion

1. Have you ever tended a garden? How is this tending similar to leadership in the church?

2. How have the organic and organizational aspects of the relationship between pastor and people been tended in your congregation? Which have been tended well? Which need tending?

Chapter 2

The Whole People of God

Phyllis C. Wiederhoeft

Because baptism is a rite of passage that many experience as an infant, we may not have memories of the experience. However, we re-live our own baptisms every time we witness a baptism. Some people also recall their baptisms daily as they shower and wash.

Adoption into God's family

Baptism is adoption into God's family through the grace and power of God's action. Adoption increases the size of a family, and a bigger family means new relationships and new roles. What becomes of the firstborn? How do the relationships between the child and each parent change? Who is who now in the family? If our congregation is the family of God, how do the relationships change as the people change—when new disciples join the family or a different pastor comes to be a leader?

Because of baptism, who we are in the family of God does not depend on any of the following:

- How we feel
- Experiencing God in a certain way
- Whether or not we struggle with faith issues and questions
- What we accomplish in our church lives or our daily lives
- Our success or our position

Phyllis C. Wiederhoeft is executive director of the Association of Lutheran Development Executives (ALDE) and a rostered associate in ministry in the ELCA.

Our identity in the family of Christ is set! We are all children of God, priests of the King, disciples of Christ, people serving others, and workers for the sake of God's mission.

Now let's be honest. How many of us have these thoughts going through our minds each time we celebrate a Baptism at worship, or each time we recall our own Baptism when we are refreshed by water? Perhaps we are like the parents in this story shared by Bishop Mark S. Hanson in his column, "Living God's Promise" (*The Lutheran*, October 2002).

> As a parish pastor I asked parents why they wanted their child baptized. After a look of shock—conveying, "If you don't know, why should we?"—they often responded, "Just in case."
>
> "Just in case what?" I would respond.
>
> "Well, just in case our baby dies," they said.
>
> "There is certainly a promise of resurrected life in Christ after death." I would explain, "but baptism isn't only for life after death but also life after birth" (p. 61).

We may not always remember that it is through Baptism that we are all called into ministry. Instead, we may think baptism is something that will get called into action later in life. This view colors the way we view the role of the pastor in our lives.

Our view of the pastor's role

The way we view baptism affects the way we view the role of the pastor in the congregation and our relationship with that pastor.

If we think of Baptism as an entry rite to go through "just in case," then we view the pastor as irrelevant in most of our lives. The pastor is there "just in case" a crisis comes up or when we want a spiritual sprinkling for good measure.

If we think of Baptism as something that's done to please other people, such as grandparents, then we view the pastor as someone who's there just doing his or her job. If we think of Baptism as the rite to gain membership in the club, then we view the pastor as the social director who's there to keep us busy and happy.

On the other hand, if we think of Baptism as God's call inviting and welcoming us into the family, then we view the pastor as a spiritual leader, set apart to be God's representative of that invitation and welcome.

We also bring our views of other leaders into church life. We look to a leader to do things for us, solve our problems, and to be there when we want her. That perspective makes the role of the leader that of a hireling: "We pay you to do what we want you to do."

This perspective often extends to the role of a pastor. Do we realize this? We use call language. We talk in the spiritual realm. Surely we don't think of the pastor as just doing our bidding. But we need to acknowledge that in our sinfulness, we far too often do want the pastor to do as we say. When we call and the pastor is not in, we wonder why not. Is she not doing her job? We might overlook the fact that she could be with a family working out details for the funeral of a loved one. When he doesn't come to my committee meeting, then why not? "He must not think much of what we're trying to do," overlooking the fact that he's visiting a mother and her children who are asking, "Who's Jesus?"

Use the "If . . . Then Questions" on page 113 to start conversations on baptism, the church, and the pastor.

Discussing our views

One of the best things that can happen between the pastor and people in a congregation is to have conversations around the differing expectations we all bring to the role of baptism, the church, the relationship we have with the pastor, and the roles we expect pastors to play. We need to get into the thick of a deep conversation about what it means for each us to be adopted into God's family, and for the pastor to be called to serve in the midst of all of us who have been set apart for service to Christ and his ministry.

The people's role

Baptism places us together, pastor and people, in a common ministry that we share as God's people:

> Now there are varieties of gifts, but the same Spirit; and there are varieties of services, but the same Lord; and there are varieties of activities, but it is the same God who activates all of them in everyone. To each is given the manifestation of the Spirit for the common good. . . . All these are activated by one and the same Spirit, who allots to each one individually just as the Spirit chooses. For just as the body is one and has many members, and all the members of the body, though many, are one body, so it is with Christ. For in the one Spirit we were all baptized into one body—Jews or Greeks, slaves or free—and we were all made to drink of one Spirit. . . . Now you are the body of Christ and individually members of it (1 Corinthians 12:4–7, 11–13, 27).

Think of our bodies and how all systems must work together for us to be healthy and function well. No one system—cardiovascular or skin or nervous system—functions without the others.

In the body of Christ, we also function together. The gifts of both clergy and laity are needed. Sometimes the pastor may be the most theologically astute person in the room. At other times, a layperson may interpret Scripture well. The pastor may help someone draw upon God for strength and hope in difficult times, while a layperson may provide understanding and communicate to someone who is struggling.

A woman in my congregation was a theologian through and through. Melanie knew scripture, Lutheran theology and polity, church history—you name it! Her most visible ministry was in a program for mothers of preschoolers as well as the Stephen Ministry. Melanie mentored untold numbers of young mothers in the ways of raising children, and in particular, raising children in the faith. She listened and comforted people who struggled with life issues and God's place in those struggles. The depth of her faith and theological understanding caused several people to encourage Melanie

In the body of Christ, the gifts of both clergy and laity are needed.

to consider the ordained ministry, but she chose to live her Baptism through her ministry within the congregation and beyond.

Called from above, within, and among

Mel Kieschnick, an associate in ministry and staff associate at Wheat Ridge Ministries, has stated that we each have a call from above, from within, and from among. He explains:

> All calls to all ministries in the name of Christ are initiated in baptism. That is indeed a call from God in which God takes God's call to all of humanity to serve God's purpose and makes it more specific. This is God's call from above to serve as part of God's "peculiar" people, the baptized.

> The call from within, then, is the spirit-directed response, desire, will, or even mandate, to use one's gifts in the service of God and God's people. This is part of the sanctified life to which the Christian heart responds and in which the growing Christian seeks to identify the specific gifts and opportunities, which converge for the daily living out of the baptismal call.

> The call from among comes from two sources: my neighbor (in both its next door and world wide context) and from the church. The call from among helps me hear the voices of encouragement from my Christian brothers and sisters and forces me to also hear my name called by the child in the Sudan, or the prisoner in the county jail, or the lonely widow next door (Mel Kieschnick to Phyllis Wiederhoeft, November 28, 2002).

Melanie showed, in all that she did, that she understood she had a call from above. God gifted her greatly through the Spirit. Melanie also knew her call from within. She responded to God's call actively through her ministry activities, reflectively through her studies of God's word, and prayerfully and joyfully in her worship life. Melanie took seriously the call from among. Those who were in community with her affirmed God's calling to serve through her vocation as a mother, mentor, and counselor.

If a pastor is *the* minister, then there's less ministry and less "status" for laypeople. Is there less status as a minister in God's family for Melanie, and countless other laypeople we can each identify? No! Ministry is not a zero-sum situation in which there are only a certain number of gifts to go around. God has given each of us different gifts and we apply those gifts in different settings, in different ways. We all are called by God to express our gifts wherever we are.

Places of ministry

Certainly the main places of ministry help define the relationship between the pastor and people of the congregation. The pastor's main place of ministry is based in the congregation. The pastor spends most of her time with activities that arise from within the congregation, such as worship, study groups, and visitations. Yet the pastor's place of ministry is not only the congregation. The pastor also seeks to be part of the community and involved in community activities, not only for the purpose of knowing the context in which his parishioners live and work, but also to carry out his vocation more fully. The pastor moves beyond the congregation when she participates in lifelong learning activities and continues her personal and professional development through study and worship opportunities outside the congregation.

The people's main place of ministry is based in the community.

The people's main place of ministry is based in the community. Members of the congregation spend most of their time with activities that arise from individual, family, and work responsibilities. Yet their place of ministry is not only in the community. The people also seek to be a part of the congregation, involved in worship and other activities in the church. They seek to keep themselves current in the study of God's Word, moving beyond a faith based only on Sunday school learning.

> "The gifts he gave were that some would be apostles, some prophets, some evangelists, some pastors and teachers, to equip the saints for the work of ministry, for building up the body of Christ, until all of us come to the unity of the faith and of the knowledge of the Son of God, to maturity, to the measure of the full stature of Christ."
>
> Ephesians 4:11–13

A balanced understanding of ministry

We come then to a balanced understanding of ministry, moving from the broad stroke of Baptism, calling us all into service, to defining our specific places and types of ministry. The beauty of our Lutheran identity is that two opposites can be held in balanced tension—godly and quite physical elements in the sacraments, divine inspiration speaking through human writers in the Scriptures, and both saint and sinner (*simul justus et peccator*) in ourselves. Likewise, we hold in balance the ordained ministry and the call to all the baptized to faithfulness, witness, and service. Pastors are called into Word and Sacrament ministry. They don't simply accept a role assigned by the community in a division of labor. At the same time, the ministry of all the baptized is not secondary to the ministry done by pastors.

We must not diminish the work of the pastor as not being "real." At some point, you may have heard someone say, "The pastor doesn't live in the real world. If he really had to work. . ." and the person went on to complain about something that convinced her that the pastor had no life experience.

We also must not diminish the work of the people as not being "real." How easily we fall into thinking that the only place our ministry and work as God's people happens is in the congregation. In this line of thinking, if we aren't serving on the council or playing piano for choir rehearsals, we aren't "really" serving God. This concept is reinforced all too often in our language and by the congregation's schedule of activities, and the "truly faithful" are expected to be at church three to four nights a week. How does that recognize the people of the congregation for serving God through other volunteer work, through being there for family time, or through confronting tough issues of ethics and responsibility at work?

The real work of ministry is done by pastors who are called to Word and Sacrament ministry, through care-giving ministries such as Melanie's, through music, educational, and staff support positions *and* through all the baptized who are called to Word and Service ministry through their lives as workers, family members, and friends in business, scientific, and artistic endeavors. The list goes on as we delineate for each other and with each other our calling from God, from within, and from among.

What works well?

If we are in conversation with each other—pastor and people—defined roles take a secondary place to a relationship of respect for each other. We acknowledge that we all have a place within God's family, not based on status, but based on the calling from God. An understanding that all of our work, lay and clergy, is real, builds a solid relationship because we build up each place of ministry rather than tearing it down. Respect for the boundaries of friendships, built on the understanding that the pastor cannot be our truest, nearest, dearest friend because of the work relationship, gives us all the freedom to serve as ministers in safe, trustworthy relationships.

Communication is vital in a relationship built on respect. It is not only that we talk with one another, helping to clarify our expectations

> " In the proper emphasis on the baptismal call for all to be in ministry to all, it can be a helpful reminder that this 'all' does include ministry to our fellow congregants. The call to 'do good,' especially to those of the 'household of faith' is a reminder to balance the commitments we make to the whole society and to the whole church as a very important part of that larger world."
>
> Mel Kieschnick to Phyllis Wiederhoeft, November 28, 2002

of each other. We also pay attention to the language we use with one another. In particular, think about the term "ministry" and its derivation, "ministers." This has been said countless times before, but bears repeating: We are all ministers. When laypeople name the pastor as "the minister," they diminish their own role as minister.

Another place to pay attention to language is in how pastors describe their call. A pastor might say, "I was called into the ministry" as though ordained ministry is it. In reality, we have other forms of ministry throughout the world—we have the ministry of all the baptized. Saying that someone has been called into *the* ministry gives a status to the calling that simply is not there.

Defining the roles of all who are in ministry keeps the relationship between pastor and people functioning well. The gifts of the Spirit are listed in 1 Corinthians 12 and Ephesians 4: apostles, prophets, evangelists, pastors, teachers, wisdom, knowledge, faith, healing, working of miracles, prophecy, discernment of spirits, various kinds of tongues, and interpretation of tongues. *The Starter Kit for Mobilizing Ministry* (Sarah Jane Rehnborg, Tyler, Texas: Leadership Network, 1994) and *Sharing the Ministry* (Jean Trumbauer, Minneapolis: Augsburg Fortress, 1995) explore these and other gifts of the Spirit.

Most importantly, pastor and people together develop their relationship as they identify, develop, utilize, and support the gifts of all the baptized. Pastors, working mainly in the congregation, can identify people's gifts for service in the congregation, provide teaching sessions for people to develop their gifts, ask and place people into the work of the congregation that utilizes their gifts, and support people as they carry out the responsibilities given to them.

We pay attention to the language we use with one another.

Yet pastors must not only concentrate on identifying, developing, utilizing, and supporting people to serve within the congregation. The task of a leader is to add value to the work of the worker for the benefit of the recipient. Therefore, the pastor's role is to be one of equipping the people for the "work of ministry, for building up of the body of Christ" (Ephesians 4:12).

What works well is the pastor remembering, and actively communicating that she understands, that the primary place of ministry for the people of God is in the community. When Steve serves on the school board, it is a vital and important place of ministry. The pastor helps equip Steve to make decisions in keeping with his identity as a member of God's family.

When pastors acknowledge the value of people serving as workers, family members, and friends, this exhibits a mutual respect for the calling from God, from within, and from among. When pastors are involved in community activities as volunteers, they too experience what it feels like to have a person or project outside of their main focus placing demands on their service and attention. When pastors value the people as ministers called to serve in the community, the relationship moves into a mutual respect for the reality that the ministry of the people is demanding, fulfilling, and rewarding.

Likewise, when people acknowledge the value of having pastors center their calling in the congregation, the relationship moves into a mutual respect for the reality that the pastor's job is demanding, fulfilling, and rewarding. That mutual respect is what works well in a healthy, functioning body of Christ, the Church.

That mutual respect is what works well in a healthy, functioning body of Christ, the Church.

For discussion

1. Describe synonyms for a "minister." Which words are proactive and which are reactive? What do these words say about the people of God who are served by a pastor? What do the words say about the relationship between pastor and people and our expectations of that relationship? What do the words say about our expectations of the laity as ministers?

2. How do we show respect for one another's ministries in the congregation and community?

3. What language do we use to describe one another's ministries? Is that language helpful? Is it a barrier to mutual respect?

Chapter 3

Expectations of Pastoral Ministry

James Kasperson

The tending of a healthy relationship between the pastor and the people of a congregation is a key to the growth of the mission of the congregation. It is also a confusing task because the role of the pastor is constantly changing with the church and our culture.

The pastor's role in a congregation may reflect the theology and background of the individual who is serving as pastor. At the same time, the congregation may have something very different in mind, based on its history of pastoral ministry. The ethnic background of both the pastor and the congregation also may influence expectations concerning the work of a pastor.

Often, roles and expectations of pastors are never articulated. When differences in understandings and expectations are not articulated and understood, conflict and disappointment develop.

In *Romeo and Juliet*, William Shakespeare wrote, "that which we call a rose by any other name would smell as sweet" (Act 2, Scene 2). Shakespeare's insight in this passage is that the essence of something remains the same regardless of the labels that we put upon it. This insight extends to our considerations of the pastoral role. A pastor is a pastor and yet we use many different names to describe the work of a pastor.

James Kasperson is pastor of Saron Lutheran Church in Ashland, Wisconsin. He has written several books on environmental education and family faith activities.

Reflecting on the variety of roles that a pastor can fill while carrying out his or her ministry can be very helpful for the pastor and members of a congregation. This chapter will assist you with that process by looking at a variety of roles, beginning with traditional understandings of the pastor and the role of the pastor compared to other models from our culture. We will see that the pastor can function in many different roles within the context of his or her ministry.

Commonly named roles of the pastor

A reasonable way to determine the general expectations that members of a congregation may have for the pastor is to look directly at what the pastor is called to do. The Letter of Call delineates many traditional and essential aspects of ministry. Other official expectations of ordained ministers are delineated in "Vision and Expectations: Ordained Ministers in the ELCA" (www.elca.org/dm/candidacy/vision_ordained.html), and Sections 7.20 through 7.47.01 (Ordained Ministry) and chapter 20 (Consultation, Discipline, Appeals, and Adjudication) of the ELCA constitution (www.elca.org/os/constitution/preamble.html). A typical Letter of Call might include the following roles.

The pastor can function in many different roles within the context of his or her ministry.

Preacher

As people of faith we see scripture as normative in matters of faith and a primary place where God reaches into our lives and calls us to live as God's people. In the role of preacher, the primary work of the pastor is to apply and interpret the living word encountered in scripture for the people of the congregation. This usually happens within the context of congregational worship, funerals, weddings, and other special services.

Teacher

This role is in many ways an extension of the preacher. The role of the teacher is to expand on the proclamation of the preacher and to provide information and education in the areas of scripture, other adult education, confirmation, first communion classes, and coordination of the congregation's education ministry.

Priest

In our tradition the pastor is the one who is designated to administer the sacraments of Holy Communion and Baptism. The role of priest includes the responsibility to teach and preserve our theology concerning these sacraments. While this role is priestly in function, the pastor does not possess any unique powers or abilities concerning these sacraments.

Prophet

This role is also an extension of the role of preacher, but it emphasizes issues of justice in the world. At times a pastor is the one who can apply a biblical concept of justice to the contemporary situation of the congregation and the world around it. This role is reflected in the Letter of Call, in which the pastor is called to "speak for justice in behalf of the poor and oppressed."

Pastoral caregiver

In this role, pastoral care (including crisis care, visitation, and counseling services) may accompany ritual functions such as funerals and weddings. Long-term counseling needs are usually referred to other counseling resources.

Administrator

This role is generally accepted as a standard duty of a pastor. As an administrator the pastor maintains and organizes the operation of the congregation, usually in cooperation with lay leaders. This role usually includes supervising staff and overseeing record keeping.

Some less commonly named roles

The common understandings of the pastor's work described above reflect a large part of the role the pastor plays in the congregation. However, additional expectations may exist in a congregation. As a result, some members of a congregation might be dissatisfied with the pastor even when commonly accepted roles are carried out. This dissatisfaction arises from varying understandings of the role the pastor is to play in the congregation.

Some expectations that a congregation places on a pastor do not fall directly within traditional understandings of a pastor's role. Both pastor and congregation can benefit from seeing the broad range of expressions that pastoral ministry can take and from seeing their own vision of ministry as only a part of that field of possibilities. Understanding the broad range of expectations may help a pastor and congregation to shape a pastoral role that is harmonious with their current partnership in ministry. At the same time, it is important for both pastor and people to understand that no one pastor can meet all of these expectations.

Look at these roles as ways to start discussion and expand understanding.

There are secular roles that can be used to articulate some of the unnamed expectations and opportunities for ministry that exist for pastors. The roles explored here each have strengths and weaknesses in describing a pastor's role. They are not offered as a complete or a definitive list, and you might want to see if you can add a model of your own. Look at these roles as ways to start discussion and expand understanding of the variety of roles that a pastor can assume and the variety of expectations that a congregation might have for the pastor. Keep in mind that an appropriate balance needs to be maintained between each of the roles a pastor assumes.

Cheerleader

The role of a cheerleader in a sports event includes naming the goal ("We want a touchdown"), focusing the attention of the community on the completion of the goal, and leading the celebration when goals

**Blessed
presence is
important
in times of
community
tragedy or
crisis.**

are accomplished. The job of the pastor is not always to be the quar-terback (doing the job) or even the coach (calling the shots) but it is to be interested and involved, sometimes from the sidelines. In times of congregational crisis pastors often have the job of identifying the problem, assisting with problem solving, and allowing qualified mem-bers of the congregation to apply the solutions.

The pastor is expected to be a voice of confidence, clarity, opti-mism, and hope within the congregation. Other people in the congre-gation are free to speak discouraging words about a given situation, but if the pastor joins in with such words the end result is either com-munal despair or frustration with the pastor.

Ambassador

The pastor is the most visible and known figure within a congrega-tion. That visibility carries with it the responsibility of representing the congregation at events that hold importance for the community. In fact, the pastor's presence usually determines a congregation's par-ticipation in ecumenical events and community services. Often the pastor is the ambassador of the congregation at area and regional events within the church–at–large.

Maintaining healthy relationships outside of the congregation can be an important part of a pastor's self-care program. In the ambassa-dor role, people expect to see their pastor involved in community organizations and activities, which can provide the pastor with oppor-tunities to develop relationships outside of the congregation.

Blessed presence

The role of spiritual leader has carried a social, interpersonal, and communal importance in many cultures throughout history. Although this weight of the office extends into our church communities, pas-tors and congregational leaders often underestimate the importance of a pastor's presence at crucial moments in the lives of people and com-munities. Blessed presence is important in times of community tragedy or crisis, such as natural disasters, major fires, or other loss of life. In times like these people historically look to the church for comfort, and the presence of a pastor—not necessarily from one's own congregation—can satisfy that need.

The blessed presence role can be important even when there is no task or apparent function for the pastor at the event. People look for their pastor at school games, concerts, and plays and invite pastors to award ceremonies, graduations, and other community-based events. Some pastoral visitation has its basis in this ministry of presence.

Midwife for life passages

The role of a midwife is to educate a woman or a couple in preparation for the birth of a child. The midwife then customarily attends the birth, as a coach for the birth process and as an expert who can recognize when trouble may develop. The midwife is usually responsible for a healthy and successful birth process, yet is not the primary participant in the process.

This model is related to the "blessed presence," but the pastor takes a more active role in the lives of members of the congregation, equipping them for many life passages including birth, baptism, confirmation, marriage, and death. The pastor teaches people or engages them in conversation before life passages including baptisms, confirmations, and marriages. The pastor also accompanies people through events. This involvement goes beyond the ritual actions associated with the passages. The pastor is often included in family gatherings that take place after a baptism, confirmation, wedding, or funeral.

The pastor teaches people or engages them in conversation before life passages.

Ritual maker

The pastor is the administrator of the sacraments of Baptism and Holy Communion. The pastor also is usually the conductor of the rites of the church as they occur in the life of a congregation, including confirmation, marriage, burial, confession, and absolution.

Along with the sacraments and rites of the church, the pastor often conducts other "ritual" events. Pastors are called upon to pray at many events of people's lives ranging from anniversaries and other celebrations to hospital and home visits with those who are sick or confined to their homes. *Occasional Services*, the *Lutheran Book of Worship* companion volume, contains many rituals used in the life of a congregation, ranging from a "Farewell and Godspeed" service for those who are leaving a community to "A Service of Healing" and "Comforting the Bereaved." These rites constitute an important part of the ritual life of the faithful, and the church continues to develop new rites for congregations to use in times of life transitions. (See www.renewingworship.org.) Within some Lutheran traditions the printed liturgies for such events are rarely used but the essence of the rituals is carried out in a less formal manner by the pastor.

Many times the role of "ritual maker" or congregational liturgist extends beyond the printed services of our church and includes pastoral leadership marking personal or community activities that are not always perceived as liturgical or spiritual. A pastor may be called upon to help individuals or families ritualize healing or progress in their lives, such as recovery from divorce or dependency. Occasionally a pastor may help an individual or family ritually celebrate a sobriety anniversary or bless houses, fishing fleets, agricultural equipment, or other important facets of life in the community.

Communities use their local clergy as ritual makers by including them in commemoration of events and dedication ceremonies for hospitals and other institutions. Although pastors were once participants in many graduation ceremonies, this now happens less frequently.

The role of ritual maker requires comfort with liturgical leadership—both formal and informal, comfort with the community, an understanding of the importance of ritual in our lives, and a creative application of ritual to specific situations.

Keeper of the story

We are a people of story. The telling of God's saving acts is the fabric of our theological and liturgical activities. As Christian people we hold the story of Christ's incarnation, ministry, crucifixion, resurrection, and ascension central to our lives as individuals and faith communities. The pastor is called to be a keeper of that divine story and this constitutes much of the traditional role of pastor.

Along with being a principal keeper of the divine story, the pastor is the keeper of other stories. Members of congregations often expect the pastor to know and keep their personal and family stories. It is important that the pastor listen carefully and attentively to these stories because they are an important point of connection for ministry to and with individuals. While it is important for the pastor to remember people's stories, it is equally important to keep the stories and maintain the confidentiality in the relationship.

The pastor is called to be a keeper of that divine story.

The pastor also becomes one of the keepers of the congregational story. When a pastor begins a new call, he or she often knows little about the congregation's past and present, but within a short time becomes a major keeper and teller of the congregational story. Pastors are often the ones who relate these stories to new members, to synodical representatives, and to the community. Knowing and telling these stories is often helpful in understanding present situations and future opportunities.

Curator of the tradition

A curator's job is to preserve the objects, documents, or ideas of a particular tradition. Pastors are called upon to preserve tradition within congregations at several levels.

First, pastors are called upon to preserve the catholic and apostolic tradition in worship and many aspects of church life.

Second, pastors are asked to be the local experts on the Lutheran tradition, including the Lutheran confessions and the official statements of the ELCA. The pastor's knowledge and understanding of these traditions can be especially helpful in times of rapid developments or conflict.

Third, the pastor is called to be mindful of the local tradition. Each congregation has a tradition that reflects many elements, including former pastors, ethnic roots, and local practices.

The pastor is often asked to strike the difficult balance between preserving all of these traditions in a healthy way that allows growth and change, or simply becoming a keeper of the status quo.

Chief executive officer

Congregational leaders may be familiar and comfortable with this model borrowed from large non-profit organizations and business corporations. The Chief Executive Officer (CEO) is a model that fits some aspects of a pastor's work, and the pastor is expected to play this role in some congregations.

A CEO in a corporation is the one person who is ultimately responsible for the entire operation. While he or she reports directly to a board of directors, the CEO supervises everyone within the organization, including the staff and volunteers. This person is expected to be familiar with all aspects of the operation and to be fluent enough in current management principles to carry out the will of the board and provide profit and progress for the organization.

Pastors who adopt this role in a congregation often benefit from using managerial and organizational skills learned from the business community. The most successful CEOs work carefully, seeking to share involvement, decision-making, and a sense of ownership with all members of the organization.

Activities director

In nursing homes, camps, cruise ships, and many other settings, the role of the activities director is important to the daily lives of residents and participants. The job of an activities director is fairly straightforward—to organize activities that are appropriate and engaging for the clientele.

The role of activities director is also important to the life of a congregation. Especially during a first visit to a congregation, people may judge the success and effectiveness of the congregation by the weekly schedule that is printed in the bulletin.

Pastors may be asked questions such as "Why don't we still have a Couples' Club?" or "Why isn't anything happening for our middle school kids?," implying that these activities are the responsibility of the pastor. The pastor may be a generator of activity ideas in many congregations, but this role can consume much time and energy if it is not shared with the congregation.

Role model

The Letter of Call includes the call to "be diligent . . . in holy living." Many expectations are expressed in this statement, including living in an ethical, moral, and exemplary manner in all facets of life.

The expectations of a congregation often extend beyond those of the Letter of Call. The pastor may be expected to model restraint, wisdom, and compassion at all times. The list is generally long, the expectations may be broad and varied, and the task is usually impossible. Pastors are often held to a super-human standard in the areas of personal and emotional management. Anger, sadness, or even extreme joy and excitement are sometimes seen as questionable when exhibited by a pastor.

It is important for pastors and congregations to remember that "holy living" is a human endeavor. It will be successful only if it is anchored in a faith that depends on God for perfection, turns to God in confession, and lives and works in a state of absolution.

One of us

At one time in our church history, pastors were chosen from within a community. Now a pastor usually moves into a community in order

Expectations of a congregation often extend beyond those of the Letter of Call.

to serve a congregation, but may still be expected to be "one of us," part of the everyday world in which members of the congregation live. In many congregations the presence of the pastor in public gathering places is an important part of ministry. This role may be fulfilled on the golf course, in a fishing boat, at town meetings, or at morning coffee in the community café. The desired result is simply the informal contact with the people of the community that results from the pastor's presence where people gather.

Corporate therapist

A psychotherapist works toward assisting a client in isolating and understanding specific areas of problem behavior, thinking, or function. Then the psychotherapist assists the client in recognizing the behavior and acknowledging it as a problem. Finally, the psychotherapist attempts to equip the client with alternative responses to problematic situations.

Congregations often have habitual responses to recurring situations. If these responses have a negative impact on the mission or life of the congregation, the pastor might take the role of isolating the problem, assisting the congregation in recognizing it as a problem, and providing healthy alternatives.

Use the tool on pages 114-115 to identify and discuss expectations and pastoral roles.

One advantage of having a somewhat mobile clergy is that a pastor entering a congregation might see and identify negative, habitual responses that seem normal to those who have been within the community for a longer time.

Using these models in congregational life

This is not an exhaustive list of role models for pastoral ministry. Your pastor may follow some other models. Your congregation may have other expectations.

Obviously no one can fill all of these role expectations. The good news is that few congregations expect a pastor to fill all of these roles.

In fact, every congregation has a unique combination of expectations of the pastor.

Pastors and congregations can use traditional and less commonly named role expectations in examining their own assumptions about the pastoral role in their settings. Call committees might evaluate the role expectations of each committee member, then use the results as an evaluative tool in their selection process. Mutual ministry committees may find these understandings useful in their work tending the relationship between pastor and people. This list of models could also be used as a congregation considers staff expansion to determine the strengths needed in a new staff person.

Disappointment or conflict can arise when there are differences in our understandings of the importance of some of these roles. The pastor may adopt a role that was helpful in a former parish but is less appropriate in a new setting. In other cases, the congregation may have too many role expectations.

If expectations are articulated in terms of pastoral roles, rather than in vague terms of disappointment with the pastor, the congregation may be able to establish a priority list of role expectations that is reasonable and attainable. When people become aware of the unconscious assumptions they have held, this is sometimes enough to persuade a change.

Every congregation has a unique combination of expectations of the pastor.

The pastor in balance

Pastors are called to lead a congregation in ministry and yet they have a responsibility to the elected leaders of the congregation. To avoid confusion, these roles must be clear to everyone.

Pastors are called to lead congregations in ministry. They come with specific skills and gifts. They have been chosen and set aside by the church to conduct that ministry of leadership within the church. They are not employees "hired" to do the will of the congregation council or the council president.

Pastors are "called" to walk together with congregational leaders and to lead in ministry. For this to happen, pastors and congregations must find a balance between two extremes, one in which the congregation or council dominates the pastor and the other in which the pastor exercises autocratic leadership.

If the balance doesn't come easily and naturally, it can still be achieved.

Each healthy relationship between pastor and people reflects a unique balance of roles and expectations. In many situations where productive and satisfying pastoral ministry occurs, the roles assumed by the pastor reflect a balance between traditional roles, the roles carried into a congregation by the pastor, and the roles expected by the congregation. Sometimes a healthy balance is achieved easily, perhaps reflecting a natural match between the pastor and congregation.

If the balance doesn't come easily and naturally, it can still be achieved. Spending the time to articulate unspoken assumptions about pastoral ministry is the first step. Recognizing and prioritizing the role expectations and gifts of pastors and congregations is the second step. Finally, this process may lead to a recognition of the broad and diverse understandings of pastoral ministry and a willingness to expand our understandings.

Pastoral ministry is not simple. Pastors are human beings with their own limitations and preconceived notions. Congregations are made up of many human beings with varied and sometimes complicated needs and expectations. Maintaining a healthy relationship between the pastor and the people requires self-examination and flexibility on the part of both pastors and congregations. An awareness of both traditional roles and expectations of a pastor and less commonly named roles can help in the process of creating a balanced ministry relationship between the pastor and the people of a congregation.

For discussion

1. In your own words, describe how the pastor carries out the roles of preacher, teacher, priest, prophet, pastoral caregiver, and administrator. What do you need to learn about these roles in order to understand them and support your pastor in fulfilling these expectations?

2. Which less commonly named pastoral roles have been emphasized in your congregation through your current pastor or former pastors? Which of these roles would you like to see increased or decreased in emphasis? Can you think of other ways to describe the pastor's role in your congregation?

3. Which less commonly named roles does your pastor seem to fill most often? Are the pastor's priorities for these roles the same as the congregation's priorities? If not, how can you best discuss these roles and priorities with your pastor?

4. What surprises have you discovered in your discussion of pastoral roles?

Chapter 4

Mutual Ministry

Rick Summy

The concept of mutual ministry and the constitutional requirement that every congregation have a mutual ministry committee (Model Constitution, C13.04) has been part of the ELCA since its beginning in 1988. The practice of mutual ministry has taken a variety of forms, but the concept is still acknowledged by most as an important aspect of the relationship between pastor and people.

What you will read in these next pages may differ from the practice and understanding of mutual ministry that you've had. If what your congregation has been doing is working, keep on doing it! If, however, your congregation has struggled with mutual ministry, this is your opportunity to take some new directions.

Definition of mutual ministry

Mutual ministry is a mission-oriented enterprise that is characterized by a broad vision of ministry and a healthy practice of mutuality.

Mission-oriented

Truly mutual ministry is mission oriented, not pastor centered. The mutual ministry committee is not the committee that ministers to the pastor or meets the pastor's personal, psychological, and spiritual needs for support, nor is it the committee through which the congre-

---

Rick Summy, an ELCA pastor and director of admissions and continuing education at The Lutheran Theological Seminary at Philadelphia, occasionally leads workshops on the topics of vocation and mutual ministry.

gation filters its complaints about the pastor. The former confuses the necessary distinction between the roles of pastor and people; the latter fosters an ineffective, often harmful approach to dealing honestly with conflict. (See Chapter 5 for healthy ways for pastors to receive support.)

Our Community provides more information on dealing with conflict.

Broad vision of ministry

Mutual ministry depends on a broad vision for Christian ministry. Simply put, ministry is service to another in the name of Christ. Christian ministry is service rendered because of Jesus Christ, and carried out in a manner consistent with what, to the best of our biblical and theological understanding, Jesus would have us do.

Lutherans understand baptism as the act by which one is called into Christian ministry. When we are baptized we become members of the priesthood of all believers. Ministry is the calling of all the baptized. Ministry is our daily work and life.

The congregation is the primary gathering of those called to ministry. The pastor plays a central, necessary leadership role in it. The pastor is responsible for preaching the Word and administering the sacraments, conducting public worship, providing pastoral care, and speaking publicly to the world.

Even so, "there is no higher status than being a baptized child of God," wrote Martin Heinecken. "Because of the office ordained ministers hold and the training they have received, they also bear a unique responsibility for the right proclamation of the gospel. *But they share*

The mutual ministry committee:

- is mission-oriented.

- builds on a broad vision of ministry and a healthy practice of mutuality.

- makes use of a small group approach to develop mutuality.

- carries out the ministry tasks of scanning and response in support of mission.

that responsibility with every Christian" (*We Believe and Teach*, Philadelphia: Fortress, 1980, p. 113, italics added).

Healthy practice of mutuality

Although this broad understanding of ministry is part of our theological heritage, many people still believe that it is the pastor who is in *the* ministry. The reasons for this gap between lay and ordained are obvious. Pastors have spent years studying the Bible and theology, learning to become articulate about the faith. So when it comes to praying in public, or leading a Bible study, or venturing a theological opinion, lay persons often defer to the pastor.

James Fenhagen has pointed to an "unconscious conspiracy" in the church: "One person (the clergy person) is allowed to feel in charge at the expense of feeling a little set apart and insecure. The other person (the lay person) is allowed to feel cared for and secure at the expense of feeling slightly inferior and with less power" (*Mutual Ministry: New Vitality for the Local Church*, New York: Seabury, 1977, p. 25). There is a kind of mutuality in this "unconscious conspiracy" but it is neither satisfying nor life-giving. A "conscious conspiracy" of healthy mutuality among pastor and people is what is needed to bridge this unfortunate gap.

Mutuality exists not "between" the pastor and people but "among" all the people, including the pastor.

All Christians are called to equip and empower one another's ministries by using the distinct gifts the Spirit has given to each one. All God's people, whether ordained or not, are called to be engaged in mutual conversation and consolation for the building up of the body of Christ and for the sake of mission.

This can be facilitated by a healthy practice of mutuality. Such mutuality exists not "between" the pastor and people but "among" all the people, including the pastor. It's mutual in the sense of being shared, working together toward a common goal.

What's the use of having a mutual ministry committee?

While a broad vision of ministry and a healthy practice of mutuality sometimes exist informally within congregations, the congregation and its mission will also benefit from a small group of people who work intentionally and intensively in ways the congregation as a whole cannot. The mutual ministry committee can concentrate on holding mutuality and ministry in creative communication, a kind of constant interplay, so that each is always seeking the other's presence.

Healthy mutuality comes through a small-group approach that takes time to nurture and strengthen relationships within the group. Such solid relationships are necessary for the sake of the ministry that the committee will do together. Healthy mutuality is not for the sake of the members themselves, though they will also benefit from it, but primarily for the sake of the ministry and mission of the congregation.

Truly *mutual* ministry will be renewing for the whole congregation, including the pastor, and will be encouraging for everyone's ministry. Truly mutual *ministry* will not serve either the pastor or the congregation, per se, but will always focus on the mission of the congregation.

Practicing mutuality: the small group, process-patient approach

Relationship building

The first six meetings of the mutual ministry committee should concentrate exclusively on building the relationships within the group. There are a number of ways to do this. One very helpful resource is *Starting Small Groups—and Keeping Them Going* (Minneapolis: Augsburg, 1995). Relationship-building exercises are also provided in the tools for this book at www.augsburgfortress.org/CLS. Feel free to discover and create your own exercises as well! Be sure to share your stories, your hopes and

Growing Together: Spiritual Exercises for Church Committees **is also a resource for building relationships.**

fears, your struggles and dreams. Be sure that everyone is speaking, listening, and understanding. Seek clarity and ask for explanations. Affirm one another as the beloved baptized children of God that you all are! The important thing is to be intentional and organized in building relationships among the members of the committee.

Process-patient

Affirm one another as the beloved baptized children of God that you all are!

We are conditioned by our culture to produce results. Committees in particular often see task as not only the primary but also the exclusive reason for being. When was the last time you were on a church committee that took the time to form relationships before it took off after its task?

Because the mutuality of mutual ministry calls for the committee to be grounded in healthy relationships, members will have to be "process-patient," that is, patient with the process of developing relationships. Members will have to put on hold their built-in desires to produce something in order to become a group in which task flows from relationship and not the other way around. This will be easier for some members than others. But if there is a healthy mix of personality types in the group—as there should be—the "doers" in the group will need to know up-front that *doing* will have to wait.

Being process-patient will enable the group to form the kinds of relationships that will lead to the best kind of *doing*. Recommendations will be looked at from different points of view. Discussions will be open and honest. Members will feel empowered to speak their own minds without fear of reproach. They will be able to have another opinion prevail without feeling it is a win/lose situation.

Being patient with the process will also enable the committee to live in the present. Any group of people that takes a significant amount of time to get to know one another without the interference of projects and deadlines is more likely to be able to avoid being trapped in the past or letting old biases or opinions infect the new relationships.

Mission focus

Although the building of relationships is crucial, so is a focus on mission. If the ministry task of the group is forgotten, the mission of the whole congregation will not benefit as intended. The committee must be mindful of this focus, even during the relationship-building phase.

Healthy relationships encourage and enable confidentiality.

Advantages

There are a number of advantages to a small group, process-patient approach to mutual ministry. Small group ministry is about working together in a way that builds a depth of relationship among the members of the group, which, in turn, enables them to work more honestly and rigorously with one another than might otherwise be expected or possible. It is the best way to build, from scratch, appropriately trusting relationships among the whole group. Everyone is involved and known. All have a part. Without any one person, the group ceases to exist.

Over time, within healthy mutual relationships, the trust and accountability that are essential for mutual ministry will develop. Where there is both trust and accountability, conflict is not a threat to either the committee or its task. Instead it is recognized as an important, even essential, component of the committee's life together. Those involved feel free to express different points of view and a rich mix of opinions are put into play.

Such healthy relationships encourage and enable confidentiality, a key ingredient in the mutual ministry mix. A committee that takes the time and makes the effort to be a group—and not just a cluster of individuals that gathers to perform a task—is likely to become a community in which betrayal is highly unlikely.

Cautions

There are also some cautions to using this approach. One is that the committee will be so good at relationship building and enjoy it so much that it will become a group for the group's sake alone. Bonding can cause a group to become stuck on itself, unable or unwilling to move beyond the confines of its safe, exciting, affirming small community.

Care must also be taken to avoid pairing off or allowing a smaller group to develop within the already small group. Factions are deadly for the trust, accountability, and confidentiality that are necessary for mutual ministry.

The mutual ministry committee is a specific kind of small group with a unique purpose.

The committee will care for its members and spend time building relationships, but the committee is not the place for crisis management or therapy. Such use of the committee can sidetrack it from its ministry task and distort its mutuality. For this reason, members of the committee should not be in crises that place them in need of extraordinary care from the pastor. This will inevitably skew the relationships within the committee.

If mutual ministry is to work, these dangers must be avoided. The mutual ministry committee is a specific kind of small group with a unique purpose in the life of the congregation. There will and should be shared ministry among members of the group. The whole point of the small group approach is for relationships to form among the members of the group. But these relationships must be among all the members.

Be realistic

No group is perfect. It's made up of human beings! No matter how careful you are in the relationship-building phase, there will likely be misunderstandings and trampled feelings. You will probably have to deal with disappointment and disillusionment. Writing about a process is one thing; living it is another. This is all the more reason to work on building the kind of relationships that can not only withstand but grow even stronger under difficult circumstances.

Even after the primary relationship-building phase is complete, attention to relationships must continue to be a part of the committee's agenda, just as a marriage relationship must continue to be carefully tended after the birth of a child if the family is to thrive.

The ministry task

Scanning

Scanning, in this context, falls somewhere in between evaluating and skimming. Think about scanning a book or magazine. You read faster than usual but not as fast as merely skimming. The idea is to get the gist of the piece without lingering too long over the details.

Imagine driving a car. As a driver you do not simply turn the key in the ignition, look through the windshield, hit the gas, and go. Although you might not always be conscious of it, once the car is started, you check the fuel and oil gauges, and make sure the windshield and other windows are clear. In other words, you prepare to drive by checking the various instruments that provide you with information related to operating the vehicle.

Once you start moving, the process continues. Even a beginner knows that you can't drive by simply looking through the windshield. Regular glances in the rear view mirror and in the side mirrors are required for driving safely. Along the way you continue to scan the instruments—checking your speed, noting the mileage, adjusting the radio, and stopping for gasoline when the tank approaches "empty." All of this scanning is necessary for a safe journey. Staring at or ignoring any one instrument for too long can cause trouble. Have you ever nearly missed being in an accident because you were adjusting the radio dial? Have you ever run out of gas because you forgot to check the fuel gauge?

Scanning is the first part of the ministry task of the mutual ministry committee. What is scanned is life within the congregation and the community. Scanning will require not only the use of your senses but also other tools that will help you to gather and interpret pertinent information about the mission of your congregation.

Attention to relationships must continue to be a part of the committee's agenda.

As you scan the ministry of the congregation, be careful not to focus just on the work of the pastor, the committees, or council. You are scanning, not evaluating! Look at the whole congregation. Look in the gaps. Glance around for needs within your community. The idea is to look at the whole picture of the congregation's mission without staring at the brush strokes. The work of the committee is more akin to a motion picture camera panning a scene than it is to looking carefully at still photos.

Ways to scan

There are a number of ways to scan the ministry of a congregation and the needs of the community.

Pay attention

Use your own abilities to look over the life of the congregation and the community. Read the newsletter and bulletins, and council and committee minutes. Read the local newspaper with ministry in mind. Read community documents that are available to you. Talk informally with members of the congregation and community. Listen to others as they share their joys and frustrations. The idea is not to focus on any particular area of ministry, including the pastor's ministry, but to gather an overall sense of life in the congregation. Is the engine overheating or simply idling? Are folks staring in the rear view mirror? Is the congregation *moving*?

Don't ask pointed questions or pretend to be a police detective. This approach will tend to make some individuals defensive and will cause others either to clam up or share more than is helpful. By all means, avoid gossip and personal gripes. The mutual ministry committee is not the congregation's complaint department! Just pay attention to what is going on.

The mutual ministry committee is not the congregation's complaint department!

Bible study

What better place to go than scripture to gain a sense of where God might be leading your congregation? How might God's action in a particular situation in scripture apply to your congregation? That's the basic question you will want to ask, even if the answer is not always easy to find or agree upon. What God is calling your congregation to do will not be clear in every instance, but remembering to ask the question may lead to some surprising conclusions.

Data

There is a wealth of information about your congregation and your community available to you via the ELCA Research and Evaluation Web site at www.elca.org/re. You'll find resources that can help you spot trends and consider whether life in the congregation and community fit together. For instance, if your community has a large number of younger children but the congregation does not have a strong Sunday school or a preschool, might that be something for the mutual ministry committee to address?

See Case Study 1 on page 118.

Response

Response to the scanning process includes a range of possibilities. The committee must not, under any circumstances, set up a program of its own or act on its own initiative. That is the congregation council's prerogative. Responses might include:

• *Sharing observations* with the council. This is a matter of simply reporting what the scanning process has picked up so far without conveying a sense that any particular action is necessary. This is a good way to share the positives, to give thanks for the gifts and strengths of the ministry of the congregation. This may also be a way to point out the initial signs of something new or unexpected.

• *Suggesting* to the council that it look into or have a conversation with the committee about a particular situation. For instance, if you were in a congregation of 150 and the pastor had conducted funerals for seven members within the past three weeks, how might your mutual ministry committee respond? This is a good example of a situation that might lead to suggestions and/or conversation with the council.

See Case Study 2 on page 119.

• *Internal discussion* among the members of the committee. So long as the pastor or the pastor's ministry does not become the primary focus of the committee's scanning, and the pastor does not seek to use the committee to support a personal agenda, there may be times when the scanning process uncovers a concern that is best discussed within the group that has worked to build a healthy mutuality. Potentially serious problems can be worked through before they ever do any damage to the ministry of the pastor or the congregation. A committee that has been carefully selected and patient in building relationships is likely to have a good deal of wisdom among its members. Use it for the good of the whole.

Any suggestion or conversation must be constructive in nature.

It is important that the committee think through these opportunities carefully. Any suggestion or conversation must be constructive in nature, an attempt to build up and not tear down. The focus must be on issues, potential for ministry, opportunities for outreach, and not on specific people or committees. It is imperative that the way the mutual ministry committee acts reflects both a broad vision of ministry and a healthy practice of mutuality.

Putting the committee together

Selection of members

While there is no way to predict how any group will function, it is almost certain that a poorly chosen group will not work. The president of the congregation council and the pastor should agree on the names of all the nominated individuals for the mutual ministry committee and the council should ratify those nominations. Keep the following guidelines in mind as members are selected:

• There should be no close friends. The relationship among all the members is paramount.

• The person serving as the liaison to the congregation council should be someone other than the pastor.

- No more than one member of the committee should be serving on the council.

- No two members of the committee should be serving together on another committee.

A variety of personality types should be reflected in the make-up of the committee. If there are too many type A ("doer") personalities, the process will be rushed. Too many type B ("being") personalities might make for a great group, but the danger is that not much will be accomplished. A mix of ages, genders, and ethnicity is desirable. One person might be someone who is less active in the life of the congregation. Such a person may offer a point of view that would otherwise be overlooked.

Be wary of volunteers for this committee. Given the prior history of mutual ministry committees which often focused on the pastor, this committee may attract volunteers who have an axe to grind, want to be "in the know," or are unable to keep confidences.

While the committee may choose to continue should a member leave, extra care should be taken when it comes time to add new members. When this happens, the committee will need to start over again with the relationship building process.

Nominees for the mutual ministry committee

The best nominees are mature and healthy, able to be and do, and to follow and lead. They should be open and excited about learning and life-enhancing change, while also being aware and respectful of the difficulty change can cause both for individuals and institutions. They need to function with unassailable integrity and to hold confidences sacred. They will need to be centered in their faith in Christ and not distracted by their own needs or biases. (See the "Would I Be a Good Mutual Ministry Committee Member?" exercise on pages 116-117.)

**Constantly
reviewing how
the committee
is functioning
is crucial.**

Trust

There must be strong trust among members of the committee, on the one hand, and between members of the committee and the congregation, on the other. The only public task this committee has is to offer the congregation council its carefully considered analysis and responses concerning the congregation's mission. There can be no suspicion of an agenda of any other kind or the committee's ministry will be compromised.

Process

Constantly reviewing how the committee is functioning is critical. No one plans to start a dysfunctional committee. Problems are more likely to slip in unnoticed through a small seed of division that gradually grows into unexpected conflict. If any one person or a smaller group of individuals within the committee begins to dominate in any way, both mutuality and ministry will be compromised. Avoiding dysfunction and domination will require constant monitoring and honest feedback at *every* meeting.

Shared leadership

Leadership is to be shared among all the members of the committee. Establishing the agenda should include input from all the committee members. The leader for each particular meeting should preside without interference from others.

The pastor will take his or her turn, but will not chair the committee. While the pastor is to be a full member of the committee, his or her needs, desires, concerns, and agendas must not be allowed to drive the committee's work.

Because the selection of the committee will have been done carefully, each member should have little difficulty taking his or her turn as the leader.

Roles

Depending on the size of your committee (five to eight members would be ideal), some or all of its members will have a specific role to play at each meeting. These roles should rotate in such a way that all perform each role an equal number of times. Schedule the roles six to eight months in advance so that everyone can prepare adequately.

At each meeting there will be a facilitator, an observer, a Bible study leader, and a prayer leader. After the initial relationship-building period, various assignments will be made with regard to the scanning process.

The facilitator

The facilitator serves as the leader for a particular meeting. With input from everyone, he or she is responsible for crafting and overseeing the agenda. The facilitator must be careful not to dominate the meeting but should keep the discussion on track and within the time-frame allotted. While allowing some room for the natural shifts of conversation, the facilitator should not allow discussion to stray too far afield.

In the beginning, when relationship building is the major agenda item, it is desirable for conversation to be freer flowing. However, even then, the facilitator will want the discussion to focus on group and relationship building and not just on interesting conversation.

The facilitator serves as the leader for a particular meeting.

The facilitator is responsible for making sure that no one person (including the facilitator) talks too much, all have sufficient opportunity to have their say, quieter members are asked for input, and each person is supported and affirmed.

Observer

While the observer is also a participant, when performing this function a person must be acutely aware of what is happening in the group on several levels. The role of the observer is to be especially attuned to the group process. He or she may wish to take notes during the meeting on the following items. (These questions were suggested by "The Leader as Observer of Process" in *Colleague 1 Program: Leader's Manual*, Chicago: Evangelical Lutheran Church in America, 1995, pp. 7-8.)

- Has someone talked too much? Too little?

- The feeling level among the group. If there was disagreement, how was that handled? Was disagreement verbalized?

- Is there tension evident among members? If so, how did it manifest itself?

- Do any smaller groups within the group seem to be forming? Are there any alliances?

- Have members listened carefully and responded appropriately?

- How is the group affecting each individual member?

- How is the group working together?

The role of the observer is to be especially attuned to the group process.

By taking notes, the observer can point to specific examples when reporting back to the committee. The observer's report enables the committee to monitor how it is working. This will help the group to make appropriate adjustments along the way to ensure that a broad vision of ministry and a healthy practice of mutuality are maintained.

Bible study leader

This person will be responsible for selecting the biblical passage to be studied and for leading the group through the study. This is sometimes an intimidating assignment, particularly if one has not led a Bible study before. Don't worry! The study is brief and there are many resources available for assistance.

Here are the specific goals for Bible study in the mutual ministry committee:

- Familiarity with and focus on scripture as foundational to our understanding of God

- Relationship building

- Inspiration and guidance for the committee's ministry task of scanning and recommending

There is no one right or wrong way to lead the study. Be yourself. Trust the other members of the group. (See the Bible Study tool in the tools for this book at www.augsburgfortress.org/CLS.)

Prayer leader

This is another assignment that may be initially uncomfortable for some committee members. It is particularly important, then, that each member be affirmed as he or she gains confidence in leading prayer. Include an opening and closing prayer in each meeting. Those who are new to this may wish to open with a prayer already written by someone else and close with the Lord's Prayer. As the committee bonds and confidence grows, prayer leaders may be willing to try some different methods. (*Starting Small Groups* is a helpful resource for leading Bible studies and praying in small groups.)

Helping the committee work

It's your committee

Keep in mind that this is your committee. Consider carefully what is written here but also think about, talk about, and decide what you believe will work best for your particular group. Make adjustments. Make the committee your own or you will never own your committee.

Before the first meeting

Each member of the committee should read this chapter before the group meets officially for the first time. Highlight what seems especially important. Let it speak to you and don't hesitate to speak back.

You may decide that you wish to do some training before the committee starts meeting on its own. Someone who is not a member of the committee or the congregation should lead the training. Contact your synod office for suggestions.

Include an opening and closing prayer in each meeting.

Ground rules

- Meet once a month for 90 minutes.

- For at least the first six months, don't meet if anyone is unable to attend. After that, make your decision about meeting without someone on a case-by-case basis. Each member is as important as every other member!

- Meet in a comfortable environment where privacy and confidentiality of conversation is ensured.

Meeting outlines

The following meeting outlines are suggestions. You will need to adjust the amount of time given to any particular agenda item. As the committee and its approach to the ministry task of scanning and recommending develops, try not to leave out any of the items. Even groups that have bonded well and have a high level of trust need to continue building their relationships, and observer reflection is integral to healthy group functioning.

During the first six to 10 meetings:
- Prayer (5 minutes)

- Sharing—using relationship building exercises (45 minutes)

- Study (20 minutes)

- Observer reflection (10 minutes)

- Review of plan and assignments for next meeting, including date, time, and place (5 minutes)

- Closing prayer (5 minutes)

After the initial relationship-building period:
- Prayer (5 minutes)

- Sharing (15 minutes)

- Study (15 minutes)

- Scanning (30 minutes)

- Observer reflection (10 minutes)

- Review of plan and assignments for next meeting, including date, time, and place (10 minutes)

- Closing prayer (5 minutes)

The first few meetings after the relationship-building period may use the scanning time to determine how the committee will approach this task. The committee may decide to work through a case study or two, to get a feel for the scanning process. (See the "Case Studies for Discussion" on page 118-119.) Divide the various assignments in an equitable way and make sure that expectations are clearly stated and understood by all. Decide ahead of time how to shape the scanning time for the next several meetings.

For discussion

1. Which aspects of serving on the mutual ministry committee are you excited about? Which concern you?

2. What opportunities does this vision of mutual ministry present for your congregation? What difficulties do you anticipate?

A prayer for the mutual ministry committee

Gracious God, open our hearts and minds to your Holy Spirit. Help us discern your will for ministry in this congregation. If our ideas and opinions prevent the adoption of your ministry, forgive us and reshape us into useful stewards of your good gifts. Merciful Lord, as we scan the congregation and community, give us insight and compassion. Keep us focused on the mission of this congregation as we decide how to respond to what we discover. And finally, eternal God, fill us with hope and joyful anticipation for the future. May the relationships we build and the work we do together in this process strengthen our congregation for ministry today and in the future. In Christ's name we pray. Amen

Chapter 5

Pastoral Ministry Support

Susan M. Lang

"It's a gorgeous day today! Have any plans for this afternoon?" asked Pastor Rush as she chatted with the Lanes during the fellowship time after worship.

"Oh, I think we'll do a little gardening," said Mrs. Lane, "we love to work outside together whenever we get a chance. What are you going to do this afternoon?"

Before the pastor had a chance to respond, she was interrupted by an emergency phone call. Whatever she had planned for the day had just changed. Two members of the congregation had been transported to the ER after a car accident on the way home from church.

Serving as pastor of a congregation is demanding and often unpredictable work. A pastor is on call 24/7, including holidays and family time. While the demands are great, the status that once accompanied the office of pastor has diminished. In addition, many people do not understand the full extent of the role of a pastor.

This chapter will examine some of the causes of the isolation that pastors often feel. The reality is that through our baptism into the

Susan M. Lang, a writer and ELCA pastor, has served in parish and campus ministry and is currently an intentional interim pastor. She wrote *Our Community: Dealing with Conflict in Our Congregation* (Augsburg Fortress).

body of Christ, pastor and people are united in one ministry and no one is ever isolated. Like a ripple in a pond, each of us is surrounded by concentric circles of support.

This chapter also describes several ways for pastors to seek out opportunities for support, growth, and development through their relationship with God, family and friends, the congregation, other professionals, lifelong learning, and the church-at-large. These options are not "shoulds" that must occur, but wonderful opportunities for pastors to meet their needs for health and wholeness.

It can be a lonely job

For a variety of reasons, a pastor can experience loneliness and isolation, even while spending a great deal of time with the people of a congregation.

Split personality?

In ordination, pastors are set apart for the ministry of Word and Sacrament: "According to apostolic usage you are now to be set apart to the office of Word and Sacrament in the one holy catholic Church by the laying on of hands and by prayer" (Ordination, *Occasional Services*, p. 193).

Being set apart to serve in the midst of the body of Christ seems a contradiction in terms, but that is the reality of the role of a pastor. The tension of being connected to others through Christ, yet set apart, is one that many pastors struggle with throughout their ministry. That setting apart carries with it many burdens and responsibilities that are not immediately obvious. This is one cause for feelings of isolation.

In strictest confidence

Pastors are the holders of confidentialities that cannot be spoken. Imagine knowing the deepest and most intimate stories of people around you and having to remember to forget them when you are in public. The burden of confidentiality, of knowing things that cannot be shared, is one that a pastor lives with each day. This is not the same as keeping secrets, instead it is holding close to your heart the stories of the individual people of God out of respect and love for them. That can be a lonely job.

Leadership is risky business

People who serve in positions of leadership sometimes act as lightning rods on behalf of the congregation. They're struck by the voltage so that it will not destroy the building or the body of Christ. Frequently when people are angry at God, they focus their anger at the pastor, God's representative and spokesperson. When change is imminent in a congregation, anger may be directed at the leaders. This is another reason why pastors might experience feelings of isolation. Few people rush to the side of a person who is under fire.

Our Community: Dealing with Conflict in Our Congregation offers many tools to prevent conflict from becoming a destructive force. Learn to identify healthy and unhealthy conflict. Recognize that dealing with conflict comes with the territory of leadership.

See *Our Community: Dealing with Conflict in Our Congregation* for more on conflict prevention and resolution.

But you only work Sundays!

If you are a lay person, chances are high that the only day you'll see your pastor is on Sundays, unless you are an active council or committee member. A lot of behind-the-scenes work occurs in the planning process. Many people don't see the details and tasks that go into preparing a sermon or organizing a worship service. They don't understand that council and committee agendas are frequently the result of previous discussion between the pastor, council president, or a chairperson. While it's a great compliment that an event can go off so well that it looks as if it "just happened," it is those kind of events that often require the greatest attention to detail.

Open conversation is needed in congregations so that everyone has a better understanding of what a pastor does during the course of the week. How is this currently handled in your congregation? What kinds of things do you ask the pastor to report? Are report summaries posted on bulletin boards or printed in newsletters? Engage in conversation so that members more fully understand the many roles of a pastor.

Some duties of a pastor serving a congregation

One of the defining characteristics of serving in ministry is that the demands are many and often unpredictable. The following list shows some of the duties that might be carried out by a pastor serving a congregation. (Actual duties will vary depending on your setting and the responsibilities designated in the pastor's Letter of Call.)

Engage in conversation so that the members more fully understand the many roles of a pastor.

Sundays
- Review sermon in advance; preach and preside at worship.
- Conduct adult Sunday school class or confirmation class.
- Attend fellowship time after worship.
- Share information and informal conversations with members.
- Follow up on emergency pastoral care. This may include hospital visitations.

Weekly
- Supervise staff.
- Respond to phone calls, e-mail, mail, and people who stop in for information or assistance.
- Prepare for and conduct a staff meeting.
- Plan worship service and prepare items for bulletin or worship folder.
- Prepare for sermon and adult Sunday school class.
- Participate in text study group.
- Conduct hospital and home visitations.

- Prepare for and lead a Bible study or confirmation class.

- Stay current on issues in the congregation, community, and world.

Monthly

- Write newsletter articles.

- Attend the local pastors' gathering.

- Meet with Bible study or small group leaders.

- Prepare for and attend meetings of the executive committee, other designated committees, and the congregation council.

- Review trend data for community and county.

Yearly

- Prepare and preside at special worship services, such as mid-week Lenten services.

- Lead first Communion class, teachers' workshops, a series of classes on a special topic, or training sessions for acolytes or ushers.

- Assist in planning a community Thanksgiving, Christmas, or Holy Week event.

- Plan a council retreat.

- Review contribution and communion records and note any increased or decreased participation by individuals.

- Represent congregation at local church, community, and synod events.

- Assist the council or budgeting committee in projecting financial contributions for the upcoming year.

- Attend synod assemblies.

- Participate in lifelong learning opportunities.

- Oversee completion of the annual report to the congregation, pastor's report to the bishop, and annual ELCA parochial report.

As needed

- Meet with prospective members and conduct new member orientation or classes.

- Meet with families planning baptisms and preside at baptismal services.

- Hold premarital counseling sessions and preside at weddings.

- Meet with people in need of immediate pastoral care.

- Pray and be present with families facing medical emergencies, the death of loved ones, or other crises.

- Prepare and preside at funeral services.

- Complete the pastor's entries on the parish register and maintain accurate parish records.

- Ensure that funds are handled appropriately.

Pastors may never know the difference they have made.

Seed planting

Much of the ministry that pastors engage in is seed planting that does not produce immediate results. In fact, pastors may never know the difference they have made, especially in a transitional setting such as interim ministry.

With the fast-paced and transient lifestyle of the twenty-first century, children seldom remain in the same communities they grew up in, parishioners come and go, and pastors move from congregation to congregation. A pastor plants seeds with congregational leaders yet may never see the harvest, and teaches children in Sunday school and Confirmation but may never know the direction the students' lives will take.

Seed planting is a job that requires faith. Pastors get their hands dirty as they dig into the soil to plant the seeds. They water what they cannot see in the hope that it will grow. Yet their job is to constantly return to the waters of baptism as a reminder that it is God who will produce the harvest. That's a promise!

Developing healthy expectations

The temptation is great when you are feeling isolated to act as if you are indeed standing alone. Pastors can easily fall into the trap of taking their responsibility to serve too seriously. This can lead to burnout and make one vulnerable to a variety of professional and sexual misconduct issues. Self-care and frequent reality checks are a wise course of action for pastors. Warning signs for the pastor include over-functioning and thinking that he or she is the only one who can do it all, violating the physical and emotional boundaries of another person, declining in physical health, or a declining or dissatisfying spiritual life.

Appropriate boundaries and mutual support

Appropriate boundaries between pastor and people are important for the health of the relationship. If either party demands too much of the other, the balance is lost. Congregations do not own pastors or pastors' time. Pastors must not expect congregations to fulfill all their needs. Healthy expectations include the following:

- Prayer, support, and encouragement for one another: This includes the congregation regularly praying for the pastor.

- Appropriate feedback: Since so much of ministry involves seed planting, constructive feedback is helpful. Some congregations have groups that meet weekly to study the Bible texts and reflect back to a pastor what they heard in the previous sermon.

- Adequate continuing education funding and time to make use of it for the pastor.

- Mutual support of spiritual renewal: While the pastor encourages lay participation in retreats and leadership workshops, the congregation encourages the pastor to have a plan for regular spiritual renewal, including plans for a sabbatical.

- Support of the congregation council and pastor for each other's ministries in the congregation and in the community: The council and pastor have a responsibility to recognize that each has a life beyond the walls of the church building. It is particularly important that pastors have a life outside the congregation so that they don't develop a dependence on the congregation.

- Support of the congregation and pastor for each other's ministries in the church-at-large: The ministry of the church-at-large requires many gifts and skills. The congregation and pastor encourage each other to share their talents with the wider church in conference meetings, synodical or church-wide committees, and synod and church-wide assemblies.

See *Our Community* and *Our Structure* for more information.

- Healthy communication skills: In healthy situations, all seek to use healthy communication skills. *Our Community: Dealing with Conflict in our Congregation* explores appropriate congregational dynamics and communications. *Our Structure: Carrying Out the Vision* discusses appropriate boundaries and accountability.

What Feeds You?

If you are a pastor, the first step to finding appropriate support outside the congregation is to become aware of the areas in your life that need tending. Use the "Tending Your Personal Growth" tool on pages 120-121 to begin to clarify the areas on which you need to concen-

---

This section will help pastors explore ways to find appropriate support outside the congregation.

trate. You might consider an annual self-review, since your needs may change over time.

As you begin to develop a plan of action to better meet your needs for health and wholeness, ask yourself this critical question: What feeds me? Self-awareness is a critical step because everyone is not fed by the same activities.

Use the Myers-Briggs typology as a tool for self-examination. Participating in groups may invigorate extroverts while depleting introverts. While judging types may thrive on organization and structure, perceiving types may need a day of spontaneity to regenerate. Once you more clearly identify your personal needs, you can discover a variety of ways to nourish your life and ministry. If you are an extrovert in an isolated area, consider attending conferences regularly. If you are an introvert and find Sundays incredibly draining, consider a private spiritual retreat for rejuvenation.

Be intentional in identifying individuals, groups, and programs that nurture you and promote wholeness in your life and ministry. The good news is that many resources are readily available. You can find

---

A thumbnail description of Myers-Briggs types

Remember that this typology merely indicates preferences for dealing with life's information in four areas. One preference is not "better" than the other, just different.

• Extroverts are fed by participation in groups and a variety of external activities. Introverts are fed by quiet time and personal reflection.

• Sensors pay careful attention to details and specifics. Intuitives play with ideas, generalities, and possibilities.

• Thinkers are logical and scientific in decision-making. Feelers are deeply concerned with how decisions will affect people.

• Judgers are structured and organized. Perceivers are creative and spontaneous.

For more information see *Personality Type and Religious Leadership* by Roy M. Oswald and Otto Kroeger, Bethesda, Md.: Alban Institute, 1988.

> While much of this book focuses on more formal means of supporting your ministry, take time to also look at less structured ways that you might be strengthened and uplifted.

nurture and support through your relationship with God; family, friends, and personal life; professional relationships; lifelong learning opportunities; and the church-at-large. Think of the options for support as a buffet. Dig in and help yourself!

Relationship with God

As a pastor and a person, you may have a wide range of relationships and lines of support, but your relationship with God is the heart of who you are as a child of God and who you are as a Christian servant. The health of this relationship is critical to the health of your ministry.

There are a wide variety of ways to nurture your relationship with God. Spiritual retreats for church leaders may be offered through your synod. There are several other resources for feeding the spirit, including the Spiritual Formation Web site of the Presbyterian Church (USA) at www.pcusa.org/spiritualformation and the Spiritual Leadership Web site of Upper Room Ministries at www.upperroom.org/fivecircles/spiritual.asp.

Spiritual companionship

Gerald May points out in his article "Varieties of Spiritual Companionship," (*Shalem News*, Volume xxii, No. 1, Winter 1998) that it is possible to have an "informal spiritual companionship" with another pastor or ministry colleague. This would involve a mutual agreement to meet and discuss how the Holy Spirit is present and active in your lives. Listening, reflecting, and discerning are all elements of these relationships.

A spiritual director

Some pastors feel called to seek a formal one-on-one relationship with a spiritual director. The term "spiritual director" refers to a spiritual guide who is willing to walk with you as you experience and discern your relationship with God. The director-directee relationship is a professional one and focuses solely on the spiritual growth of the directee. How does the Holy Spirit move and work in your life? How can you be more receptive to the Spirit as you live? These are the questions at the heart of spiritual direction.

How does the Holy Spirit move and work in your life?

Both the Shalem Institute for Spiritual Formation and Spiritual Directors International are resources as you search for a trained spiritual director in your area. (See the Recommended Resources on pages 111-114 for more information.) Group spiritual direction is also a possibility for three to five clergy who decide to support one another in their spiritual growth.

A sabbatical

The sabbatical is another means by which pastors can take time for spiritual and vocational renewal. A sabbatical is an intentional time set apart for renewal, reflection, rest, and reconnecting with the Holy Spirit's activity in your life and ministry. The focus of a sabbatical can be anything that uplifts and reinvigorates you and your ministry, such as travel, development of hobbies, educational pursuits, and intense spiritual reflection.

Begin with a dream for renewal. Several resources can help you make it happen. See *Clergy Renewal: The Alban Guide to Sabbatical Planning* (Bethesda, Md.: Alban Institute, 2000) for a complete sabbatical plan, including sample education pieces for the congregation, brochures and policies, personal goal setting, and program and financial resources. Some synods have sabbatical guidelines posted online at www.elca.org/dm/leadership/sabbatical.html. In addition, the Charis Ecumenical Center at Concordia College, Moorhead, Minnesota (www.cord.edu/dept/charis) offers a guide to sabbatical planning and an extensive list of resources, including grant sources and program centers. The Lilly Endowment National Clergy Program (www.clergyrenewal.org) also offers funding.

Honoring the Sabbath

A basic way to focus on your relationship with God is to begin the practice of honoring the Sabbath. Pastors work on Sundays so they must respect days off, family time, and vacation days. Be intentional. Practice stewardship of body, mind, and spirit. Take care of yourself.

A pastoral care covenant

Pastor Garcia sits alone by the bedside of his wife, who has just returned from a life-threatening surgery. He is so filled with worry that words of prayer elude him.

Who pastors the pastor?

Few people consider that many pastors do not themselves have pastors during times of personal and family crisis in the same way that members of a congregation do. While synod staff members can be a valuable means of support, their schedules and duties are already extensive. Who pastors the pastor?

Consider forming an intentional covenant with a colleague to ensure that you and any family members have pastoral care at all times. Don't wait until a crisis strikes you, your family, or your ministry. When that time comes, you'll be glad you know who to call and your colleague will support you with his or her prayers and presence.

Remembering who you are

A pastor is also a child of God. The temptation is great to get so caught up in serving and doing for others that you forget you are also part of the baptized body of Christ. That means you are never alone. God's love surrounds you, too. Always.

Family, friends, and personal life

Years ago, the church was a gathering place for all community activities and recreation. There was little else. While that has changed for most people, the pastor is particularly susceptible to having no life outside the church building. What happens when a pastor moves on to another call or retires? Will the pastor or her family be forced to begin everything anew because of a lack of outside friends and interests?

As set apart yet serving in the body of Christ, pastors must not rely upon the congregation to meet all their needs. This means that you must attend to the development and maintenance of close personal relationships outside the congregation. Get together with friends weekly or monthly. If you're married, go out on regular dates with your spouse.

Think about your interests and take time to pursue them.

Include family time in your weekly schedule. If someone wants to meet with you during that time, you have the right to tell that person you're already booked. Your family needs you, too, through all the rites of passage, triumphs, and struggles of life. Elderly parents often need assistance. Children grow quickly and life is short. Live your life in celebration of the times you've spent together, not in regret of the things you've missed.

What feeds you? Think about your interests and take time to pursue them. Look for hobbies and interests outside the church. Get involved in community projects. Volunteer to coach youth sports teams. Local school districts or community colleges often offer a variety of courses in everything from computers, to dance, to woodworking. Start a book discussion group. Learn to play an instrument. Activities outside the church will help you maintain a healthy balance in your life and will strengthen your ministry.

Examine your schedule. Are there areas in which you are currently lacking? How might you carve out more time for family, friends, and non-church activities? Go ahead, get a life! You'll be happy you did.

Professional relationships

Pastors do a lot of listening on the job. As a result, you need safe places where you have the opportunity to talk—places where you can share your fears and frustrations and where you can develop ideas and dream. Let's look at some of the options open to pastors for collegiality and professional support.

Colleague groups

For years, pastors have gathered in pericope or text study groups, convocations, continuing education workshops, and fellowship events for mutual support. As a result of the effectiveness of the ELCA Colleague program to support and encourage the newly ordained, there has been an increased emphasis on also developing Colleague programs for those more experienced in ministry. *Refuge*, a 14-minute video discussing the Colleague Program as implemented in the Northeastern Iowa Synod, is available in all synod offices. See the Recommended Resources on pages 109-112 for other Colleague program materials. The Colleague program's ecumenical materials can be valuable resources for groups that include pastors from other faith traditions.

The formats for colleague groups vary. Groups may be theme-based and gather pastors of like interests such as senior pastors, those in rural ministries, and those with interests in spiritual growth or evangelism or even secular interests such as camping and hiking. In the Northeastern Pennsylvania Synod, groups were created to match experienced pastors with those newer to ordained ministry.

The Alban Institute has initiated The Clergy Collegium, a new program to facilitate interdenominational support. Contact Alban Institute for information on future groups.

You may also choose to connect with colleagues in discussion groups via the Internet. Luther Link (www.lutherlink.org) provides monitored discussion threads reserved for responsible participants.

A coach

Since the mid-1990s the field of career and goal coaching has exploded with the formation of coaching schools and formal accreditation. In their book, *The Spiritual Leader's Guide to Self-Care* (Bethesda, Md.: Alban Institute, 2002), Rochelle Melander and Harold

Lifelong learning

Opportunities to continue your education through lifelong learning can help you learn or enhance skills and re-energize your ministry, often while getting acquainted with colleagues. Life Long Learning Opportunities (www.faithandwisdom.org), a ministry of the Episcopal Church USA, ELCA, and United Methodist Church, provides a searchable Web database of learning opportunities throughout the world. The ELCA also provides a Web directory of lifelong learning partners and continuing education centers at www.elca.org/dm/lllcenters.html.

SELECT offers resources for use with small study groups. Topics include biblical studies, history, liturgy, the Lutheran confessions, evangelism, and preaching. Visit the Web site at www.elca.org/dm/select for a full course list and additional information.

Eppley write from a coaching model. They define coaching in this way: "It is about making and embracing changes, maintaining well-being, and fixing problems in the present and the future. Once information is gleaned, the question is always, 'Now what?'" (p. xiv).

Coaching generally takes place through phone and e-mail, so your coach can be located literally anywhere. The frequency and duration of sessions is negotiated.

Since coaching is action and results oriented, it is important to have a clear understanding of your personal and professional goals when you obtain a coach. Are you unsure about how to escape the stress cycle? Do you need help in preparing for interviews with call committees? Define your greatest need and search for an appropriate and compatible coach. Sources for locating coaches include the Christian Coaches Network, Coach U, Coachville, and the International Coach Federation. See the Recommended Resources on pages 109-112 for more information.

The therapeutic relationship

Is your job affecting your relationships at home or vice versa? Perhaps the personal and vocational load that you are carrying is too great and you need to explore why you are feeling overwhelmed. Perhaps your kids are acting out. Don't overlook the possibility of seeking a trained counselor or therapist. Benefit plans through the ELCA Board of Pensions give you access to mental health, chemical dependency, legal, financial consulting, and wellness services. Many synods also offer ministry assistance programs to refer pastors and their families to appropriate counseling sources. Check to see what's available. Remember you're human and everyone needs to unload burdens every now and then.

The church-at-large

The Body of Christ extends far beyond the walls of your church building. Pastors are messengers of Christ called to serve the people of God. That call extends beyond your doors, too. Involvement is expected at conference meetings, pastors' gatherings, and synod assemblies. Frequently pastors are called upon to share their leadership skills and individual talents with synodical or church-wide committees. There are also increased opportunities for ecumenical gatherings, dialogs, and pulpit exchanges among those churches that are full communion partners.

Summary

Pastor and people—we're in it together! We serve our Lord Jesus Christ in all we do, both word and deed. Let us strive to develop strong relationships and circles of support so that the seeds we plant may sprout, grow, and flourish. Let's do our best to encourage a fruitful harvest in Jesus' name.

Networking and engagement with the church-at-large can energize a local ministry with fresh ideas.

For discussion

1. Why do pastors often feel isolated in their role?

2. What can congregational leaders do to encourage the pastor to seek appropriate support in carrying out their call to ministry?

3. As pastor and people, what are your current expectations of one another? Are they healthy and appropriate? If yes, then how can you nurture those expectations? If no, what can you do to move to a healthier relationship?

4. As a pastor, where are you finding your strongest support? Which circle of support are you currently lacking in your ministry and personal life? How can you develop a plan of action?

Chapter 6

Ministry Review and Performance Evaluation

Martha W. Clementson

One of the most common questions from congregational leaders calling a synod office is, "Do you have something we can use to evaluate our pastor?" The caller may be motivated by the belief that the pastor is not carrying out ministry adequately, or by the hope that difficulties in the working relationship between the pastor and people can be avoided by putting an evaluation process into place early enough. In almost all cases, congregational leaders readily admit that they have no idea how to begin doing a pastoral evaluation.

On the other hand, pastors raise concerns about the way most evaluations are conducted. One pastor says, "When I hear about a pastor being evaluated, it makes me anxious because I've seen this done poorly or maliciously much more than I've seen it done well and positively." Another pastor points out, "A basic flaw in most pastoral evaluations is that they place responsibility for the 'success' of the parish only on the pastor."

Added to this, pastors and lay leaders generally assume that everyone has mutual goals for ministry and common expectations of one another. However, in reality they are often operating with different visions and values.

Martha W. Clementson, an ELCA pastor, has served as assistant to the bishop in the Southwestern Pennsylvania Synod since 1987, working with congregations, pastors, and rostered lay leaders in times of conflict, pastoral transition, and mission planning.

A fair and realistic process

Conducting a fair and realistic evaluation of ministry is important for every congregation. A ministry review takes into consideration not only the leadership qualities of the pastor, but also the ministry provided by lay leaders and members of the congregation. This builds a foundation for performance evaluation through prayer, conversation, and team building. Once a congregation establishes a ministry review and performance evaluation process, periodic checks can help to keep the ministry on track. An annual review process can become an essential routine for healthy congregations of all sizes.

This chapter provides a process congregations can use to accomplish the following:

- Clarify role expectations between the pastor and congregational leaders.

- Conduct a performance evaluation that assists pastors to see themselves through the eyes of others, giving them the opportunity to build on strengths and address weaknesses.

- Give congregational leaders an opportunity to consider the level of lay participation in the congregation's ministry.

- Build a common vision for ministry with goals that inform the work of both pastor and laity.

Preparing for a ministry review and evaluation

The day of a new pastor's installation is a high point in the life of a congregation. Once the installation celebration is over, congregations and pastors are faced with the daunting task of living up to their expectations of one another. The writer of 2 Timothy recognized that people will not always stay focused on the Gospel of Jesus Christ:

> In the presence of God and of Christ Jesus, who is to judge the living
> and the dead, and in view of his appearing and his kingdom, I solemnly
> urge you: proclaim the message; be persistent whether the time is favor-

able or unfavorable; convince, rebuke, and encourage, with the utmost patience in teaching. For the time is coming when people will not put up with sound doctrine, but having itching ears, they will accumulate for themselves teachers to suit their own desires, and will turn away from listening to the truth and wander away to myths. As for you, always be sober, endure suffering, do the work of an evangelist, carry out your ministry fully.

2 Timothy 4:1-5

Our own personal desires may very well get in the way of doing the ministry and mission that God places before us. We may not only wander away from sound doctrine, but we may have very different understandings of how we should go about carrying out God's ministry fully. Chapters 2 and 3 show the many and varied expectations that we carry with us about ministry and the roles of a pastor.

Develop mutual expectations

Conversation with one another will help clarify our expectations and assist us in reshaping unrealistic expectations into workable and productive goals, and can also help us recognize and address the changes and challenges faced by every congregation and community over time. As the years go by, lay leaders and pastors need to continue to find ways to talk honestly with one another about the congregation's ministry and the ways in which the pastor and people are carrying out that ministry.

Conversation with one another will help clarify our expectations.

Establish a foundation

A firm foundation must be established before a fair and realistic ministry review and performance evaluation can even begin. The foundation is formed out of a shared understanding of the purpose and focus of the congregation's ministry and a common understanding of lay and pastoral roles. A number of resources can help to shape this mutual understanding, including the *Model Constitution for*

Congregations of the Evangelical Lutheran Church in America. (An online version of the Model Constitution is available at the Office of the Secretary Web site at www.elca.org/os.)

Constitutional responsibilities

The Model Constitution identifies the leadership responsibilities of both pastors and congregation councils and serves as a guide to the ministry to which God has called each of us. A pastor is called to the responsibilities listed in the constitution, regardless of the geographic location or size of a congregation. Likewise, every council is charged with constitutional duties.

The constitutional responsibilities of a pastor and lay leaders highlighted in C9.03, C9.12, and C12.04-C12.09 not only overlap in some areas, but can only be carried out effectively in partnership with one another. For example, the pastor is called to preach the Word, administer the sacraments, conduct public worship, provide for pastoral care of members, offer instruction, and promote the mission of the wider church. While these are primarily responsibilities of the pastor, they are not done in a vacuum. Therefore, the pastor must work with the traditions and expectations of the local community of believers in shaping the specific ways in which these responsibilities are carried out. Likewise, the council has the primary responsibility to lead the congregation in stating its mission and goals, which cannot be done effectively without the participation of the pastor. The pastor and council are both called to carry out administrative responsibilities. In addition, the constitution calls on both lay leaders and pastors to work together to promote unity, remain centered on God's love for the world through Jesus Christ, and develop a ministry that will be inviting to those who are not yet a part of the church.

The focus of ministry

Healthy, growing congregations today realize that the church exists primarily for the sake of sharing the good news of God's love in Jesus Christ with people who are not yet active in the body of Christ. This focus of ministry is different than that of stagnant and declining congregations, where ministry centers only on the comfort and satisfaction of the current membership. It is therefore important to ask this question during the annual ministry review, "Are we placed here by God primarily for ourselves or also for the sake of others?" If the answer is "also for others," the time and energy of the pastor and council will need to focus on leading the congregation forth in mission.

"Are we placed here by God primarily for ourselves or also for the sake of others?"

Gather input

Conversations about ministry and leadership roles can be greatly enhanced through the participation of another local pastor, the synod bishop, or a member of the bishop's staff. Such individuals can help you establish a foundation that is faithful to the vision of the constitution, connected to the realities in the world, and mindful of the needs of pastor, congregational members, and persons yet to be invited into the faith. They can also bring a broader perspective and knowledge about ministry in other contexts.

Three components of review and evaluation

While congregations share much in common, each one also takes on its own unique shape. The process for making decisions, the people who need to be involved, and the timing varies from congregation to congregation. A review and evaluation process needs to be shaped in such a way that it works for the congregation. As you shape the process in your congregation, you will want to be certain that three things are included: ministry goals, performance evaluation, and planning for the next year.

Ministry goals

A council member in a midsize congregation reported, "What we do at St. John's is to bury hurts and anger to protect the pastor. We avoid discussing problems with the pastor's performance or treatment of others, I think, not only because we want to protect him but also because there is no common ground on which to begin. Consequently, because of our inability to deal with even the most basic issues, hostility runs rampant under the surface and hurts from years ago remain in the mix. When issues finally do come to the surface, there is an eruption and reconciliation may be impossible."

For more discussion on mission and goals, see *Our Mission: Discovering God's Call to Us* and *Our Context: Exploring Our Congregation and Community.*

Before a fair and helpful ministry review and performance evaluation can take place, leaders must have a common vision for the ministry of the congregation. This provides "common ground" for discussion. Therefore, the first step in a ministry review and performance evaluation is to identify the goals on which the ministry is operating.

Begin by finding out whether your congregation has identified ministry goals. Goals identified during the call process are placed on the Statement Form of the call document after the pastor is called. In some congregations, long-range planning committees or other groups identify ministry goals. In other congregations, the congregation council develops ministry goals each year. (If your congregation does not have agreed upon ministry goals, use the tool on page 126 to begin the development of ministry goals.)

The "Reviewing Ministry Goals And Achievements" tool on page 122 provides a format for discussing specific ways in which the pastor and laity have endeavored to carry out each goal. The ministry review also involves discussing whether each goal needs to be continued.

Performance evaluation

Because of the intertwining roles of pastor and people in the congregation, it is important that the review and evaluation include mutual conversation about the understanding of ministry held by the pastor, staff, and laity. This is also a time to identify specific ways in which ministry is being carried out. Use the "Performance Evaluation" tool on pages 123-125 to enable conversation about how well the pastor and laity are performing in basic ministry areas. These categories allow for discussion of local needs while also evaluating ministry in light of the wider church's expectations.

Planning for next year

The final step in an effective ministry review and performance evaluation process is planning for the next year. To shortchange this step would make the process incomplete. Furthermore, there would be no basis for a future review of ministry.

Provide ways for those conducting the ministry review to be in dialogue with the group that sets ministry goals in your congregation. The people involved in the review and evaluation could assist in the goal-setting process by identifying specific ways in which the pastor, staff, and laity will work to carry out ministry goals. If there is no process for establishing ministry goals in your congregation, those performing the review and evaluation could develop goals and recommend them to the congregation council for adoption. The "Developing Ministry Goals" tool on page 126 provides a process for doing this.

Getting the job done

The congregation council is charged with the responsibility "to lead this congregation in stating its mission, to do long-range planning, to set goals and priorities, and to evaluate its activities in light of its mission and goals" (C12.04a). Further, working with staff and volunteers to see that ministry is carried out effectively and helping the pastor and staff "annually evaluate the fulfillment of their calling" is part of the work of the congregation council (C12.04.c and C12.04.d). Yet, most councils do not take the time to engage in an annual ministry review process.

For a variety of reasons, the full congregation council may not be able to devote the time needed for a fair and productive ministry review and evaluation process each year. Therefore, most congregation councils would do well to assign the ministry review to a specially designated group of people. In this chapter, that group will be called a "ministry review team."

The best time to begin a ministry review is when you think that you do not need one!

Empower a ministry review team

The congregation council can appoint a ministry review team to the specific task of conducting the ministry review and performance evaluation process. The use of a special team can prevent role confusion, broaden participation, and bring together representatives from various groups involved in the congregation's ministry. Depending on the size of your congregation, a team of six to 12 members is appropriate. The pastor is a full participant in the process. If the congregation is served by additional pastors or rostered lay leaders, they are full participants as well.

Make ministry review an annual event

To keep the focus on the ministry itself, the ministry review is not connected to the congregation's budgeting process. In fact, it is ideal to conduct the ministry review and the budgeting process at different times of the year. The entire review and evaluation process normally takes no more than four to six weeks. Don't drag it out!

The best time to begin a ministry review is when you think that you do not need one! In an editorial in the journal *Congregations* (March/April 2002, Volume 28, Number 2, Alban Institute), Lisa Kenney wrote, "Here at the Alban Institute we have noticed that many people who contact us struggle with doing evaluation. Unfortunately, when someone calls our consulting or research departments concerning this topic it is often too late to help them evaluate effectively because they already have a problem: the issue of evaluation has been raised only because of perceived shortcomings or controversy about the pastor's leadership. This is not the time to bring it up" (p. 3). Make ministry review and performance evaluation a regular annual event instead.

Present a report to the council

Once the review has been completed, a report is submitted to the congregation council for its adoption. Use general statements rather than those that are too specific, especially if the recommendations involve areas needing substantial improvement. This report summarizes:

- how ministry goals are being carried out by the pastor, lay leaders, and congregational members.

- areas of strength and areas of concern in the performance of pastor and laity.

- ministry goals for the coming year, including initial steps that will be taken by pastor and laity to achieve these goals.

Council members may amend the report before it is adopted. It may be appropriate for the council to refer this report to its executive committee for action. Once the council has acted, the report is shared with the congregation so that all can participate in carrying out the ministry plans. The council thanks members of the ministry review team for their service and disbands the group.

Tailoring the process to your congregation

- If your congregation shares the pastor with one or more congregations, share your final reports with each other at a joint council meeting.

- If your congregation has more than one pastor, include all pastors in the process, giving attention to each pastor's particular areas of responsibility. (The Letter of Call will specify duties in settings with more than one pastor.)

- If your congregation has additional staff members, particularly a person on one of the lay rosters, include consideration of that person's responsibilities in the process.

- If your congregation is a new mission start or a redevelopment, invite the ELCA Mission Director for your area to be involved in the review and evaluation process.

- If your congregation has been through a high level of conflict, invite your synod bishop or a member of the synod staff to be involved in the review and evaluation process.

Ministry review team agenda

• Identify previous ministry goals and discuss the ways in which the pastor, staff, and laity have carried out these goals.

• Conduct the performance review assessing how well pastor and laity have provided leadership based on the goals.

• Agree upon ministry goals for the next year (or work with the planning group responsible for goal setting) and identify specific ways in which pastor and people will work toward achieving the goals.

• Present a report of the ministry review and evaluation to the congregation council.

Follow through

At various points throughout the year, the council should take time to examine how the plans made in the ministry review process are being carried out. This can be especially helpful when the ministry review uncovered specific areas of concern. It may be helpful for the council to include a "ministry review update" in its agenda at least once each quarter in order to provide the support needed to follow through on the actions that were agreed upon.

Turn to others if you need help

Don't forget that your synod bishop and staff are partners in your ministry. Ask them for help if you believe that you could benefit from an outside facilitator. Also ask for help if you run into concerns that you cannot address on your own. Someone from the synod staff, a trained volunteer provided by the synod, or another consultant may be available to help you conduct a review and evaluation in an open and fair manner, if you feel unable to do so. Assistance in defining a vision for mission and writing ministry goals is usually available from the synod as well.

If a congregation and pastor have reached a high level of conflict, a ministry review and performance evaluation process is not appropriate or helpful. If your congregation is in this type of situation, seek help from your synod bishop or a church consultant.

A tool for working together

The ministry review and evaluation process serves as a tool to discuss expectations and forge a common work ethic for both pastor and people. It lays the groundwork and provides checkpoints to prevent differences from turning into major issues. The process can be most effective when used on a regular basis.

In 1 Thessalonians, Paul expresses a high regard for those who lead in the church and calls on us to work harmoniously for the common good: "But we appeal to you, brothers and sisters, to respect those who labor among you, and have charge of you in the Lord and admonish you; esteem them very highly in love because of their work. Be at peace among yourselves" (1 Thessalonians 5:12-13).

We need to have open and honest conversations on a regular basis in order to live out the New Testament's vision of Christian ministry. Every congregation and pastor will benefit by getting into the habit of working from a common vision and talking together about ministry openly, honestly, and frequently.

For discussion

1. How do differences in expectations between the pastor and lay leaders get worked out in your congregation?

2. In your congregation, is the ministry focused primarily on the care of current members or on the extension of the congregation's ministry into the community? How does this focus impact the daily work of the pastor and congregational leaders?

3. In what ways does your congregation believe that the "success" of the ministry depends upon the pastor? In what ways does your con-

gregation believe that the "success" of the ministry depends upon the laity? What is the level of lay involvement in carrying out the ministry? How do the laity and pastor work together as a team in your congregation? How could the laity and pastor better work as a team in your congregation?

4. What is the process for setting annual ministry goals in your congregation? What factors get in the way of following through on ministry goals?

5. How would your congregation benefit from the appointment of a ministry review team? What time frame for a ministry review and performance evaluation would work best for your congregation?

6. What would need to be done in order to establish or maintain a ministry review and evaluation process that would be helpful to your pastor and congregation?

A prayer for the ministry review team

Gracious God, open our hearts and minds to your Holy Spirit. Help us discern your will for ministry in this congregation. If our ideas and opinions prevent the adoption of your ministry, forgive us and reshape us into useful stewards of your good gifts. Merciful Lord, as we evaluate one another and ourselves, give us insight and compassion. Enable us to speak with both courage and gentleness. And finally, eternal God, fill us with hope and joyful anticipation for the future. May the work we do together in this process strengthen our congregation for ministry today and in the future. In Christ's name we pray. Amen

Chapter 7

Personnel Committee

Leonard C. Larsen

Michael R. Rothaar

Introduction

Congregations of the ELCA are independently incorporated. Unlike Lutherans elsewhere in the world or other denominations in the U.S., ELCA congregations can own property, manage their own finances, and employ their own workers.

Being responsible

The congregation needs the same kind of procedures and policies that any other organization would have, whether or not it is organized for profit.

The personnel committee is the group in the congregation that carries out the obligations of the congregation as an employer. In some large congregations this may be a standing committee that meets regularly. In smaller congregations a personnel committee may meet only occasionally. Personnel work may even be carried out by another com-

---

Leonard C. Larsen has consulted with pastors and multiple-staff teams for 37 years. During his 17 years as president and CEO of Lutheran Social Service of Iowa, he was closely involved in personnel management.

Michael R. Rothaar, an ELCA pastor, serves in the ELCA Division for Congregational Ministries (DCM). He coordinates planning, communication, and resource development. Before joining the churchwide staff in 1987, he served congregations in Ohio and Michigan.

mittee, such as the finance or the executive committee, that devotes part of its agenda to these issues. If this is the case in your congregation, the committee must identify those times when it is carrying out personnel functions so that these issues are handled separately.

A personnel committee makes recommendations to the congregation council rather than making decisions or establishing policies on its own. The *Model Constitution for Congregations* of the ELCA calls upon the congregation council:

Members of the personnel committee need to understand their work as a ministry of justice.

> To oversee and provide for the administration of this congregation to enable it to fulfill its functions and perform its mission (C12.04.c).
>
> To maintain supportive relationships with the pastor(s) and staff and help them annually to evaluate the fulfillment of their calling or employment (C12.04.d).

The role of the personnel committee, however it is formed, is to assist and support the congregation council in carrying out these responsibilities.

Being fair

Members of the personnel committee need to understand their work as a ministry of justice. The committee has a special obligation to be sure that the congregation is fair to the people it pays to carry out its work. There is a corresponding obligation to see to it that employees provide the services for which they are paid.

As an organization, if the church does not follow fair and just practices with regard to its personnel and someone is harmed, the congregation can be sued in a court of law. There can also be other repercussions. However, avoiding lawsuits or protecting the congregation's assets—while important—are not the highest and best motivations for the work of the personnel committee. The theme of justice is much more important and more central to the nature and mission of the church. Being fair—doing what is just—should be the core mission and common commitment.

The pastoral epistles in the New Testament are evidence that already in the first century concerns similar to those we experience today had arisen. Paul, for example, wrote to the congregation in Thessalonika, Greece, about how enthusiastically they had greeted him when he visited and committed themselves to the proclamation of the Gospel. At least two passages in these epistles are pertinent to the work of the personnel committee:

1. Paul reminds the Thessalonians that when he was with them in person he earned their support of him with "labor and toil." He mentioned that because, apparently, some people had begun expecting payment without work as though they were entitled to it (1 Thessalonians 2:7-12).

2. He implored or beseeched them to "respect those who labor among you" and "esteem them very highly in love because of their work" (1 Thessalonians 5:12-13).

We can't easily draw parallels between our congregations and those of the first century. Customs, laws, traditions, and cultures are very different. But it isn't that difficult to see that broad principles apply to both. Writing to Timothy, Paul mentions the "elders who rule well" (1 Timothy 5:17) and tells him that they are worthy of honor, especially "those who labor in preaching and teaching." (The word translated as "elders" is *presbyteros*, which is the root of the office known as "priest," which among Lutherans is the office commonly known as "pastor.") In discussing what is owed them, Paul cites from Scripture, "The laborer deserves to be paid" (1 Timothy 5:18).

Being partners

In relation to the pastor, the functions of the personnel committee are somewhat different than with staff members. (Another book in the Congregational Leader Series, *Our Staff*, deals more comprehensively with the congregation's responsibilities with staff members.)

In a mutual ministry committee (Chapter 4), common understandings can be developed and both the congregation's and the pastor's ministry goals can be carefully examined. A ministry review team

**See *Our Staff:*
Building Our
Human
*Resources.***

(Chapter 6) can help the pastor to annually review his or her contribution to the work of the whole church, and to develop ways to strengthen effectiveness in service. The work of the personnel committee is related but different.

See the
"Checklist
of Personnel
Issues"
on pages
127-128.

- The personnel committee is responsible for annually reviewing all compensation provided for the pastor, and seeing to it that appropriate action is taken by the congregation council regarding such compensation.

- The personnel committee is also responsible for other issues with legal implications, such as ensuring, as much as possible, that the congregation is providing a safe and secure working environment.

- The personnel committee will work with all parties involved to be sure that lines of authority are clear, and that employees are enabled to carry out those aspects of ministry that have been entrusted to them.

Living up to the agreement

The unique nature of the relationship between pastor and people can be difficult to understand and the literature the personnel committee considers can be confusing. The government, for example, will tend to refer to the pastor as an *employee* of the congregation at some times. But when there is consideration of social security issues, the pastor will be referred to as *self-employed*.

Members of personnel committees may find it easy to incorrectly put the pastor in the role of "employee." However, a more appropriate way for the personnel committee to view the relationship between pastor and people is to see the pastor as a *professional with a service contract*. Although no analogy is perfect, there are examples from other spheres of society. Your optometrist or veterinarian may be a professional with a service contract, if he or she is not in private practice. Under a service contract, the doctor would work for a large corporation and would be paid by the corporation to carry out professional services. However, the corporation does not pay doctors according to *how* they practice medicine. If the corporation says, "You must pre-scribe Brand X vitamin for every patient," it has overstepped its bounds. The corporation as employer does not determine what good medical practice is.

This is similar to the situation of the congregation through its personnel committee. Compensation is provided for an ordained ELCA pastor to carry out ministry under the auspices of the particular congregation. But the pastor is not an "employee" of the congregation in the everyday sense of the word, with the employer directing how particular functions are to be carried out. As a result, this book sepa-rates the functions of compensation planning and evaluation. Lutheran pastors are expected to do certain things. Congregations are expected to support them—financially and in other ways.

Lutheran pastors are expected to do certain things. Congregations are expected to support them.

Annual review of compensation

Salary

An agreement about the responsibilities of the congregation in obtaining the services of the pastor already exists in the Letter of Call, which is a contract. The first part of the agreement lists the profes-sional services that are expected. The second part of the agreement, which spells out the expectations for compensation and other matters, is what concerns the personnel committee. The Letter of Call specifies that this section be reviewed annually.

Clergy compensation is a somewhat complicated matter that includes salary, medical benefits, provision for retirement income, continuing education, and other benefits. In comparison to other pro-fessions, clergy compensation is unique in including provisions for the pastor's home as well.

Synod guidelines

Although each congregation is separately incorporated and carries out its own responsibilities, the task of the personnel committee is made easier by the fact that compensation decisions are made in concert with other congregations. This helps to promote fairness and ease of decision making. First, the synod brings together a committee of people with expertise in personnel issues to formulate suggestions. Then all congregations are represented at the Synod Assembly, where part of the agenda each year is to act upon the committee's recommendations and establish guidelines for compensation.

Synod guidelines typically take into account a variety of factors: years of experience, comparison to other synods, scope of responsibilities, local economic factors, and so on. Typically a chart is created to show ranges of salary for the variables used. The personnel committee simply takes these guidelines—approved by all the congregations acting in concert—and inserts the appropriate figures into its own congregation's spending proposal.

Some congregations find the guidelines too low for their situations, and wish to pay the pastor more. They are free to do so. It is advisable, though, to think through why this might be done. Because there is a tendency to mistakenly think about clergy compensation as "a reward for work well done," some denominations are careful not to describe the compensation of pastors as "salary" or "pay." Rather, they speak of

A pastor may be willing to receive compensation below the synod guidelines, but the personnel committee should carefully examine and probably resist this temptation. For example, the pastor may be independently wealthy, not needing compensation from the congregation to make a living. However, budgeting for a reduced amount of compensation may habituate the congregation to that level. When the independently wealthy pastor moves elsewhere, it may be difficult to reconfigure the budget to a more realistic level of compensation. It would be better to pay the independently wealthy pastor the "going wage" and allow him or her to make charitable contributions outside the congregation with the excess.

the "support" of clergy. Pastors receive just compensation on par with other pastors and sufficient for them to live and support their families. This support is not a favor or a "reward."

Some congregations, when reviewing the guidelines approved by the synod assembly, believe that they should be allowed to pay their pastor at a lower level. They are wrong. All synods approve their guidelines at a *minimum* level. These levels are not negotiable.

If a congregation believes that the synod guidelines do not meet its needs, the personnel committee initiates a conversation with the synod's bishop or compensation committee to discuss the situation and explore the issues involved. In the case of a congregation that claims it can't afford to provide appropriate support for a full-time pastor, the bishop may recommend seeking a part-time pastor or sharing the office with another congregation.

All synods approve their guidelines at a *minimum* level. These levels are not negotiable.

Housing

Most people choose where they live based on how much they can afford to pay. Members of the personnel committee will have to take into account that this issue is more complicated for pastors.

Some congregations provide housing and expect the pastor to live there. This arrangement prevents the pastor from incurring a loss in order to serve the congregation. (Although this is done in some other denominations to expedite moving pastors from one setting of ministry to another, this is not the case in the ELCA.) Providing housing or a parsonage is appropriate for congregations in settings at the extremes of the economic range. In high-income communities, property is so valuable that the congregation would have difficulties providing sufficient income to make it affordable. In other communities, real estate is in such low demand that a pastor would be unlikely to recoup the investment in a home.

When the congregation provides housing for the pastor, it should assume all the responsibilities that a landlord normally has with regard to a tenant. (All of the usual restraints upon a landlord should be regarded as if they apply as well.) In these instances, the personnel committee carries out its functions best by consulting with a real estate agent or attorney who works with rental properties, and developing a document similar to a lease agreement. This document would spell out the mutual responsibilities of both parties, although no "rent" would be due from the pastor. The expectations for other housing costs (such as utilities) need to be specified in writing.

Many congregations choose to provide compensation adequate for the pastor to provide his or her own housing. The synod guidelines may have suggestions for how this amount is to be calculated, but may not list specific figures.

The housing allowance is not considered taxable income to the extent that it meets IRS requirements. Generally, the housing allowance includes the cost of principal and interest payments on a mortgage (or full rental costs), insurance, taxes, maintenance, and repairs. Synods often suggest that congregations consult with local real estate specialists to determine average amounts for such expenses. The congregation can determine whether it wishes to contract for a figure above or below such estimates. The personnel committee should review the contracted figure regularly to determine whether it is appropriate in light of actual costs.

For tax purposes, a housing allowance is separate from the salary figure. It does not have to appear that way on the congregational budget, but there must be separate supporting documentation for tax purposes. The congregation, through the congregation council, must annually state in writing what amount of the total compensation is designated as clergy housing allowance. The personnel committee must ensure that a written record of this decision is kept on file, enabling the congregation to respond to inquiries from the IRS.

The chief advantage of a housing allowance is that it allows the pastor to build equity in a home, which will be of benefit at a future time (such as retirement) if housing is not supplied. As with any investment, there is a risk that housing values may decrease rather than increase. The congregation is not expected to indemnify pastors against such risks.

Supplementary compensation

When housing is provided or when only rental properties are available in the area, many synods recommend that the congregation supplement the pastor's salary with an equity allowance. Because this amount is often intended to benefit the pastor after retirement, consideration should be given to using a tax-deferred method of making this payment.

Clergy are treated as self-employed and the congregation does not make the employer contribution to the pastor's Social Security account. In addition, when clergy compute the self-employment tax due they must include the value of their housing allowance or home provided by the congregation. Because this has the effect of reducing the spendable income of clergy below the actual amount paid, many synods recommend that the congregation provide an additional allowance to make up the difference.

The health and wellness benefits provided by the ELCA are sound, but not necessarily comprehensive. There may be different medical insurance needs with respect to dependents or to coverage under other plans (such as a spouse's employer). Some congregations provide benefits beyond those required, such as supplementary insurance for medical, dental, disability, and long-term care needs.

Decisions about supplementary compensation of any kind have legal and tax implications for the pastor. These decisions should be based on up-to-date authoritative information, not on the brief treatment in this book. The synod compensation committee may provide information and suggestions and the ELCA Board of Pensions makes a wealth of information available on its Web site (www.elcabop.org). As such agreements are established through the Letter of Call and annually reviewed, they should be discussed with the pastor, who should consult with his or her own independent advisors.

Some congregations provide benefits beyond those required.

Annual review of benefits

ELCA benefits

On behalf of the pastor, the congregation contributes a percentage of the compensation to the ELCA Pension and Other Benefits plan. A packet is available for congregational treasurers to compute and submit the congregation's payment.

The ELCA benefits program is designed to help provide a lifetime of financial security for pastors, rostered laypersons, lay employees, and their families. The program provides flexible health, retirement, disability, and survivor benefits coverage to meet the changing needs of plan members.

Although the personnel committee may wish to review what is required of the congregation, there are no decisions to make regarding the ELCA benefits plan unless the pastor's situation is so unique that further advice is needed from the Board of Pensions. The personnel committee should, however, evaluate whether the congregation is meeting its responsibilities, such as ensuring that all payments are being made in a timely way.

Time away from the congregation

Chapter 5 in this book explores how pastors balance the varied responsibilities of pastoral ministry with personal and family responsibilities. The personnel committee, along with the mutual ministry committee, can be an advocate for the pastor when there are misunderstandings about the responsibilities of pastoral ministry. These committees can help to clarify that the time the pastor spends occupied with ministry outside the congregation (such as attending the synod assembly, serving on boards or committees of the wider church or its institutions, or undertaking special interfaith projects) is part of his or her ministry, not to be designated as "personal" time.

The personnel committee deals with the more formally and contractually recognized time away, including budgetary expenses for pastoral services provided by a substitute. The Letter of Call for the pastor specifies that there shall be four weeks of annual vacation. The personnel committee should also decide, in dialogue with the pastor, how to address other time off: a designated weekly day off, holidays, sick leave, family needs, bereavement, and so on. Synod guidelines may include specific suggestions for how such time should be designated. There seems to be a trend in some places, for example, to regard all such leave as "personal days," and leave it up to the pastor to use the time as needed. Generally, there are limits to how many days (if any) can be accrued from year to year. If synod guidelines do not suggest appropriate types or amounts of time off, the congregation's personnel committee might wish to consult with other congregations or organizations to determine what is customary in the area.

Issues can arise, and well-written policies provide a basis for dialogue.

Many congregations have no formal policy on the expected work week and leave time for the pastor. When there is a good and productive mutual ministry between pastor and people, this is rarely a problem. But issues can arise, and well-written policies provide a basis for dialogue when either the pastor or the congregation feels that the other partner in the relationship is treating them unfairly. The personnel committee can support the work of the mutual ministry committee and ministry review team by developing a clear set of expectations. When misunderstandings and conflicts arise, only those expectations that have been mutually agreed upon in written form can serve as an effective basis for conversation or mediation.

Continuing education

Professionals in many fields are expected to participate in continuing education. When the ELCA accepts a person on its roster of ordained pastors, it expects the person to continue to learn how to be effective in his or her work and to grow in knowledge and understanding for the sake of the Gospel and the people served. The expectation is for at least 50 "contact hours" (the equivalent of time spent in a classroom) annually, or 150 hours over a three-year period. As

The 1997 ELCA Churchwide Assembly adopted a "vision and strategy statement" concerning continuing education, titled "Lifelong Learning and Development for Faithful Leaders." This overview is available on the ELCA Division for Ministry's Web site at www.elca.org/dm/leadership/life_long.pdf. Links to other helpful resources for the personnel committee (including sample guidelines from synods) can be found at www.elca.org/dm/documents.html.

part of the call to a pastor, the congregation agrees to provide time and financial support for this endeavor.

The synod compensation committee may have suggestions for the personnel committee to consider. Typically, 14 days of continuing education annually are suggested. The congregation may budget a grant for this purpose. The congregation is expected to provide $700 annually and the pastor $300, as long as all money is spent exclusively on the cost of continuing education, including tuition, room and board, and travel. In the case of pastors serving in their first call, participation in First Call Theological Education (FCTE) is required and this additional expectation is reflected in the Letter of Call.

A congregation also might support continuing education for the pastor by designating a set amount for work-related books and subscriptions to publications.

Beyond the annual continuing education time and subsidy, the ELCA suggests that there be provision for a "sabbatical," or an extended study and renewal period. This may be a period of one to three months, and should take place every three to five years that the pastor has served under the call to the congregation.

There are tax implications for the pastor regarding all continuing education allowances. Competent advice should be secured regarding the most favorable ways in which these subsidies can be provided.

Non-financial or administrative compensation

The personnel committee should explore ways in which the pastor's compensation can be addressed without incurring additional expenses for the congregation outside of administrative time and effort (including, perhaps, a change in the way the congregation's books are kept). Among other sources, the ELCA Board of Pensions regularly makes information available about such allowable benefits. (Visit www.elcabop.org and see information on clergy taxation under "benefit plans.") For example, a pastor may ask that his or her salary be reduced by an amount to be deposited to a tax-deferred account or a "medical savings account." The money then comes "out of the pastor's pocket" before he or she receives it, which requires the congregation to take additional steps. Obtain professional advice to be sure all requirements are met.

Reimbursements

The Letter of Call specifies that the pastor is entitled to receive reimbursement for expenses incurred on behalf of the congregation. The personnel committee ensures that there are forms and procedures in place for submitting reports of reimbursable expenses and making reimbursements in a timely way. Such reimbursements are not compensation, but contractual obligations of the congregation, paid to a person carrying out work on its behalf.

If the pastor picks up the choir robes from the dry cleaner and pays the bill out of his or her own pocket, no rational person would even think about including that reimbursement in the budget under the pastor's salary and benefits. Yet it is still all too common to see a line item for car allowance under that category.

Although a few congregations may wish to provide an automobile as part of the pastor's overall compensation (in which case the car's value may be taxable income), for most congregations, what is meant by "car allowance" is the use of the pastor's own car for carrying out the church's business. The IRS has clear rules pertinent to all employees—not just pastors or other church employees—about this expense. At a minimum, documentation is required to show that the expense claimed is attributable to carrying out the business of the employer (activities performed in the course of employment, like making hospital calls, but not commuting between home and office). Synod guidelines will probably suggest the most appropriate method of reporting and computing this reimbursement in a way that meets IRS guidelines.

A safe working environment

No one enjoys discussing this topic, but pastors (and staff members and volunteers) are sometimes harmed by other people in the course of carrying out their responsibilities. And pastors (and staff members and volunteers) sometimes harm other people in an abuse of the privilege of their position.

The personnel committee is responsible for developing policies and procedures that seek to protect people from harm. The church must never put people at risk, and must do everything possible to diminish potential risks. As discussed earlier, this is primarily a justice issue, not a matter of protecting the congregation from lawsuits. The personnel committee should also work with other appropriate congregational leaders to be sure that insurance coverage (worker's compensation and liability) is adequate to protect the congregation's assets in cases where the policies and procedures aren't sufficient to prevent the harm.

It is beyond the scope of this chapter (and book) to make specific recommendations for such policies. For some general information that will be useful to the personnel committee in consulting with the congregation's own attorney and insurance agent, see www.elca.org/dcm/ministry_planning.

The congregation is not alone in dealing with issues that arise. The congregation is not alone in dealing with issues that arise. The synodical bishop, when informed about an allegation, will inform you of steps to take in response. Consider, for example, an allegation of sexual harassment. (In the context of personnel policies, this means a demand or expectation of sexual gratification as a condition of employment, but it may also be construed more broadly.) The "first responder" may be the personnel committee, the congregation council or its executive committee, or some other individual or group. The important thing is that the complaint be taken seriously and immediately carried forward to people prepared to deal with it. The allegation *must not* be ignored, minimized, "investigated" by congregational leaders, or discussed without synodical and legal consultation. No person or group within the congregation may take it upon themselves to give assurances, either to the victim or perpetrator, or take any action without counsel from competent authority.

The personnel committee should regularly review the working environment for conditions that might lead to harm. Are offices used for counseling, for example, completely shielded from view? Or are building security and maintenance neglected in ways that may lead to victimization?

A brief resource like this book cannot anticipate every question or prescribe the right answer for every case. The personnel committee's general responsibility is to ensure that these guidelines are followed:

- Every person who works for the church should know to whom they can report situations that put them at some kind of risk. This might be the pastor, the congregational president, the chair of the personnel committee or someone else.

- Every person who reports a concern should be confident that the person or group that hears their concern will report it to someone with greater responsibility. (There is no expectation of confidentiality that is to be created.) In the case of allegations of criminal behavior, the congregation will strictly adhere to legal requirements.

- Every person who reports a concern will be informed about the action that is taken in response.

- A confidential file will be created to document the occurrence and the steps that are taken by representatives of the congregation.

The personnel committee should regularly review the working environment for conditions that might lead to harm.

Accountability, communication, and authority

When more than one pastor is serving a congregation, the Letter of Call to each pastor will specify their individual duties and expectations. The personnel committee, in conjunction with other congregational leaders, should regularly review such professional relationships to see that they are harmonious and productive.

> How can the personnel committee possibly know whether conditions are "safe?" Checklists and guidelines will be of some help. But the most important guide you have is the pastor or staff person who says, "I don't feel safe."

As discussed more fully in *Our Staff* and *Our Structure*, the pastor functions as the "chief executive officer" of the congregation and normally is the supervisor of the staff. With regard to lay employees of the congregation, the personnel committee must see to it that supervisory authority is clear, and that employees are not forced to confront conflicting expectations.

The personnel committee can help others in the congregation understand that no individual or group within the congregation (such as the congregational president or the congregation council) has supervisory authority over the pastor. The hope is that through a positive mutual ministry process, differences of opinion, when they occur, can be resolved.

See *Our Staff: Building Our Human Resources* and *Our Structure: Carrying Out the Vision.*

The person who has the responsibility of overseeing the ministry of the pastor and congregation is the synodical bishop. Consult chapter 8 of the *Constitution for Synods of the ELCA* (available online at www.elca.org/os/constitution/synodcon.html) for a variety of applications of this principle. For example, note these excerpts:

S8.12. As this synod's pastor, the bishop shall be an ordained minister of Word and Sacrament who shall:

a. Preach, teach, and administer the sacraments in accord with the Confession of Faith of this church.

b. Have primary responsibility for the ministry of Word and Sacrament in this synod and its congregations, providing pastoral care and leadership for this synod, its congregations, its ordained ministers, and its other rostered leaders.

h. Practice leadership in strengthening the unity of the Church and in so doing:

1) Exercise oversight of the preaching, teaching, and administration of the sacraments within this synod in accord with the Confession of Faith of this church;

2) Be responsible for administering the constitutionally established processes for the resolution of controversies and for the discipline of ordained ministers, other rostered leaders, and congregations of this synod.

The congregation's own governing documents also provide a framework for understanding and further developing the accountability structure. These include the constitution (which cannot conflict with the *Model Constitution for Congregations* of the ELCA found at www.elca.org/os/constitution/intro.html) and continuing resolutions that may be adopted to clarify how the congregation entrusts selected people to carry out its ministry.

Provide information about personnel issues to all concerned.

Unfortunately, there are times when relationships break down and when an individual's service is deemed unsatisfactory. The constitutions of the congregation and synod, as well as other personnel policies that may have been developed, are the framework within which the personnel committee must proceed. Fairness to all parties involved is of paramount importance, and is the reason for establishing clear procedures (including, as appropriate, the right of appeal).

Because the congregation is a voluntary association (and not only a nonprofit corporation), it is especially important to provide information about personnel issues to all concerned. In cases where controversies arise, the personnel committee can advise the congregation council about appropriate official statements. It is important for the congregation to be transparent to all involved parties as it deals with its staff, even while keeping confidential those matters that should not be public.

Many conflicts among staff members, and between the staff and members of the congregation, occur because it is not clear who has authority to make decisions. The personnel committee can facilitate better understanding by reviewing and revising the position descriptions developed for the staff. Organization charts are sometimes helpful in communicating accountability to the congregation as a whole.

For discussion

1. Obtain a copy of the latest action by your synod assembly on clergy compensation. Identify areas that require further study or a change in your congregation's present practices.

2. Review all non-confidential documents in your congregation's personnel files, including the Letter(s) of Call and position descriptions. Also review your congregation's constitution, especially those chapters that deal with the pastor and the congregation council.

3. Invite your congregation's attorney and insurance agent for a conversation about issues that arise from employment law in your state or area. If no one on the personnel committee deals with personnel issues in their daily work, identify another member of the congregation who does this type of work to sit in on these conversations.

4. As the personnel committee, find out who in your congregation serves as the mutual ministry committee and the ministry review team. Meet together and discuss how the roles of each group are different, and how each can support the others.

A prayer for the personnel committee

Gracious God, open our hearts and minds to your Holy Spirit. Help us discern your will for ministry in this congregation. If our ideas and opinions prevent the adoption of your ministry, forgive us and reshape us into useful stewards of your good gifts. Merciful Lord, enable us to deal fairly with people the congregation pays to carry out its work, so that they can carry out their responsibilities as productively as possible. Give us insight and courage for this ministry of justice. And finally, eternal God, fill us with hope and joyful anticipation for the future. May the work we do together strengthen our congregation for ministry today and in the future. In Christ's name we pray. Amen

Recommended Resources

Books

Arnold, Jeffrey. *Starting Small Groups: Building Communities that Matter.* Leadership Insight Series. Nashville: Abingdon, 1997.

Berry, Ewin. *The Alban Personnel Handbook for Congregations.* Bethesda, Md.: Alban Institute, 1999.

Bullock, A. Richard, and Richard Bruesehoff. *Clergy Renewal: The Alban Guide to Sabbatical Planning.* Bethesda, Md.: Alban Institute, 2000.

Cloud, Henry, and John Townsend. *Boundaries: When to Say Yes, When to Say No, to Take Control of Your Life.* Grand Rapids, Mich.: Zondervan, 1992.

Colleague Program: Colleague 1 Leaders Manual and Synod Handbook, Colleague 2 Facilitator's Manual and Synod Handbook, Division for Ministry, Evangelical Lutheran Church in America. Ecumenical guides for both programs also available. Order from the ELCA Distribution Service, Augsburg Fortress, Publishers, P.O. Box 1209, Minneapolis, MN 55440-1209, phone: 1-800-328-4648.

Congregational Leader Series. Ten volumes. Minneapolis: Augsburg Fortress, 2002-2003.

Congregations newsletter, Bethesda, Md.: Alban Institute, March/April 2002. This issue focuses on evaluations.

Dougherty, Rose Mary. *Group Spiritual Direction: Community for Discernment.* New York: Paulist Press, 1995.

Foss, Michael W. *A Servant's Manual: Christian Leadership for Tomorrow.* Minneapolis: Fortress Press, 2002.

Halaas, Gwen Wagstrom. *Ministerial Health and Wellness Report, 2002, Evangelical Lutheran Church in America.* Evangelical Lutheran Church in America, 2002. Report available online at www.elca.org/dm/health.

Hammar, Richard R. *2002 Church and Clergy Tax Guide and CD ROM Set* (updated annually). Charlotte, N.C.: Church and Tax Law, 2002.

Hedahl, Susan. *Listening Ministry: Rethinking Pastoral Leadership.* Minneapolis: Augsburg Fortress, 2002.

Hudson, Jill M. *Evaluating Ministry: Principles and Processes for Clergy and Congregations.* Bethesda, Md.: Alban Institute, 1992.

Johnson, George S., David Mayer, and Nancy Vogel. *Starting Small Groups—and Keeping Them Going.* Minneapolis: Augsburg Fortress, 1995.

Kallestad, Walt. *Turn Your Church Inside Out: Building a Community for Others.* Minneapolis: Fortress Press, 2001.

Kirkpatrick, Thomas G. *Small Groups in the Church: A Handbook for Creating Community.* Bethesda, Md.: Alban, 1995.

Mead, Loren. *The Once and Future Church: Reinventing the Congregation for a New Mission Frontier.* Bethesda, Md.: Alban Institute, 1991.

Melander, Rochelle and Harold Eppley. *Growing Together: Spiritual Exercises for Church Committees.* Minneapolis: Augsburg Fortress, 1998.

Melander, Rochelle and Harold Eppley. *The Spiritual Leader's Guide to Self-Care.* Bethesda, Md.: Alban Institute, 2002.

Meyer, Richard C. *One Anothering, Volume 2: Building Spiritual Community in Small Groups.* Philadelphia: Innisfree, 1999.

National Assembly of National Voluntary Health and Social Welfare Organizations. *Screening Volunteers to Prevent Child Sexual Abuse: A Three-Step Action Guide.* Washington, DC: National Assembly of National Voluntary Health and Social Welfare Organizations, 1997.

Nessen, Craig. *Beyond Maintenance to Mission: A Theology of the Congregation.* Minneapolis: Fortress Press, 1999.

Olson, Mark. *Moving Beyond Church Growth: An Alternative Vision for Congregations.* Minneapolis: Fortress Press, 2002.

Oswald, Roy. *Clergy Self-Care: Finding Balance for Effective Ministry.* Bethesda, Md.: Alban Institute, 1991.

Oswald, Roy W. *Getting a Fix on Your Ministry.* Bethesda, Md.: Alban Institute, 1993.

Payne, Claude E. and Hamilton Beazley. *Reclaiming the Great Commission: A Practical Model for Transforming Denominations and Congregations.* San Francisco: Jossey-Bass, 2000.

Rehnborg, Sarah Jane. *The Starter Kit for Mobilizing Ministry.* Tyler, Texas: Leadership Network, 1994.

Rubietta, Jane. *How to Keep the Pastor You Love.* Downers Grove, Ill.: Intervarsity Press, 2002.

Savage, John. *Listening and Caring Skills in Ministry.* Nashville: Abingdon, 1996.

Sitze, Bob. *Not Trying Too Hard: New Basics for Sustainable Congregations.* Bethesda, Md.: Alban Institute, 2002.

Trumbauer, Jean. *Sharing the Ministry.* Minneapolis: Augsburg Fortress, 1995.

Turner, Nathan W. *Leading Small Groups: Basic Skills for Church and Community Organizations.* Valley Forge, Pa.: Judson, 1996.

Warren, Rick. *The Purpose Driven Church.* Grand Rapids, Mich.: Zondervan, 1995.

Willimon, William. *Pastor: The Theology and Practice of Ordained Ministry.* Nashville: Abingdon, 2002.

Woods, C. Jeff. *User Friendly Evaluation: Improving the Work of Pastors, Programs and Laity.* Bethesda, Md.: Alban Institute, 1995.

Organizations

Alban Institute: Suite 1250 West, 7315 Wisconsin Avenue, Bethesda, MD 20814, phone: 301-718-4407 or 1-800-486-1318, Web site: www.alban.org.

Christian Coaches Network: phone: 425-558-1845, Web site: christiancoaching.com.

Coach U: P.O. Box 2124, Salina, KS 67402-2124, phone: 1-800-48COACH, Web site: www.coachinc.com.

The International Coach Federation: 1444 "I" Street Northwest, Suite 700, Washington, DC 20005, phone: 888-423-3131, Web site: www.coachfederation.org.

Lilly Endowment National Clergy Program, 2801 North Meridian Street, P.O. Box 88068, Indianapolis, IN 46208-0068, Web site: www.clergyrenewal.org.

SELECT: 2199 East Main Street, Columbus, OH 43209-2334, phone: 614-235-4136 Ext. 4021, Web site: www.elca.org/dm/select.

Shalem Institute for Spiritual Formation: 5430 Grosvenor Lane, Bethesda, MD 20814, phone: 301-897-7334, e-mail: info@shalem.org, Web site: www.shalem.org.

Spiritual Directors International: 329 Seventh Avenue, San Francisco, CA 94122-2507, phone: 415-566-1560, e-mail: office@sdiworld.org, Web site: www.sdiworld.org.

Web sites

Congregational Leader Series: www.augsburgfortress.org/CLS.

ELCA Board of Pensions: www.elcabop.org.

ELCA Division for Congregational Ministries, Ministry Planning: www.elca.org/dcm/Ministry_Planning.

ELCA Division for Ministry: www.elca.org/dm.

Life Long Learning Opportunities: www.faithandwisdom.org. This searchable database is a ministry of the Episcopal Church USA, Evangelical Lutheran Church in America, and United Methodist Church.

Alban Institute and the Indianapolis Center for Congregations. Congregational Resource Guide: www.congregationalresources.org.

Chapter 2 Tool

If . . . Then Questions

The following questions could be used over the course of several meetings. Choose one or two at a time to discuss in a group.

1. If you expect higher morality from your pastor, then what do you expect from other leaders?

2. If pastors saw themselves as shepherds, then how would they see members of a congregation?

3. If most congregation members knew more about most things than the pastor, then what would happen?

4. If you encouraged someone to consider ordained ministry as a vocation, then how would you characterize this calling?

5. If pastors thought of themselves as administrators of programs, then how would they define success?

6. If pastors only performed those tasks that help members of congregations to do their daily life ministries, then what would pastors stop doing?

7. If you were to name the five biggest misconceptions about the ministry of the people, then what would you list?

8. If you were to name the five biggest misconceptions about the pastor's role, then what would you list?

9. If_____, then_____?

10. If_____, then_____?

Some of these questions were adapted from Bob Sitze, Director for Congregational Stewardship Development, ELCA Division for Congregational Ministries.

Chapter 3 Tool

A Look at Pastoral Roles

Use this tool in your congregation council, call committee, mutual ministry committee, or other group that works with the relationship between pastor and people to discuss your perceptions of pastoral roles.

Ask each person to complete questions 1 through 3 on their own. Responses to question 3 could be shared in small groups. Work on step 4 as a large group.

1. You have 50 points to distribute throughout the following list. In Column A, distribute the points based on your own understanding of the needs of your congregation at this time.

2. Think of a pastor who had a positive effect on you. In Column B, distribute 50 points based on your understanding of the roles carried out by this pastor.

3. Compare your responses in Column A and Column B. What effect, if any, did your responses in Column B have on your "ideal" list in Column A?

4. In Column C, attempt to distribute 50 points in a way that reflects group consensus. Consider inviting your pastor to participate in this process.

	Column A	Column B	Column C
Preacher			
Teacher			
Priest			
Prophet			
Pastoral caregiver			
Administrator			
Cheerleader			
Ambassador			
Blessed presence			
Midwife for life passages			
Ritual maker			
Keeper of the story			
Curator of the tradition			
Chief executive officer			
Activities director			
Role model			
One of us			
Corporate therapist			
Other: _____			

Chapter 4 Tool

Would I Be a Good Mutual Ministry Committee Member?

Discernment exercise

Read Romans 12, 1 Corinthians 12, 2 Corinthians 4, and Ephesians 4. In light of these texts and your knowledge of yourself, answer the following questions:

1. Do I keep confidences easily?

2. Am I able to speak my mind in a diplomatic way?

3. Am I truly a team player?

4. Am I patient enough for a lengthy process of relationship building?

5. Am I willing to tackle difficult tasks?

6. Do I have the time, or will I make the time, to give mutual ministry adequate attention?

7. Am I good listener?

8. Am I able to both lead and follow?

9. Am I willing to let go and trust the Holy Spirit?

10. Am I able to consider the well-being of the whole life of the congregation?

11. Am I open to having my mind changed?

12. Am I willing to speak up when I disagree with what others are saying?

No one will be able to honestly answer "yes" to all of these questions. After prayerful consideration of these questions, if you can answer most of them with a strong affirmation, then you have a good chance of being an effective member of the Mutual Ministry Committee.

Chapter 4 tool

Case Studies for Discussion

Case study 1

Your congregation is one of the few remaining viable congregations in a small town that has experienced significant population loss and economic difficulty for the past 50 years. The pastor is capable but a bit inexperienced, the third first-call pastor in a row for the congregation. The average attendance at worship is 130, while the average age of the members is 55 plus. The Sunday School still provides classes for kindergarten through junior high or middle school, but the classes are grouped together because of the small number of children. There is virtually no day care or pre-school available in town.

The mutual ministry committee has reviewed recent census data, which reveals an influx of new families, most with young children, into new housing being built on former factory sites on the outskirts of town. There are many two-income households in this new development and most of the residents commute to a nearby medium-sized city for work.

How does your mutual ministry committee deal with this information? What do you discuss? Is there other information you might wish to gather? Are there people with whom you want to talk? How will you respond?

Case Study 2

Your congregation is very active and averages about 150 at worship each week. The pastor is widely acknowledged as both a hard worker and a family person.

In the past three weeks, an unusual number of congregational members have died—seven all told. One was a young child who died of sudden infant death syndrome. One was a mother in her mid-thirties who died of cancer. A car accident claimed an active teenager's life. Four were elderly, including two who had been confined to their homes due to health. All four had been as involved in the congregation as their circumstances allowed.

A week after the last funeral, the Mutual Ministry Committee meets, and the unusual number of deaths comes up in discussion.

Use your imagination and discuss how the committee might respond should this happen in your congregation, keeping in mind that mutual ministry is about the ministry of the whole congregation.

Chapter 5 Tool

Tending Your Personal Growth

Self-assessment for pastors

1. Read 1 Timothy 4:14-16.

2. For the following six areas of health and wholeness, think about what you are currently doing. Are there areas in which you're currently not doing anything? Write down your thoughts in the "Reality" column.

•Spiritual: Your personal and corporate relationship with God, including prayer, study, contemplation, and reflection.

•Physical: Attention to health, nutrition, and exercise and avoidance of abusive behaviors.

•Emotional: Management of stress and mental health.

•Social: Healthy relationships with partners, children, and/or friends, and learning how to love deeply and knowing that you are loved. A healthy support system is essential for this area of health and wholeness.

•Vocational: Accepting your call to ministry and recognizing, developing, and using your gifts.

•Intellectual: Intellectual growth through participation in lifelong learning, study, and challenging conversations.

3. What do you need to discard, either because it hasn't worked or is no longer serving your growth needs? Write down your thoughts in the "Weeds" column.

4. What do you need to seed for the future? In which direction would you like to go? What is your dream or vision? Write down your thoughts in the "Seeds" column.

	Reality	Weeds	Seeds
Spiritual			
Physical			
Emotional			
Social			
Vocational			
Intellectual			

The six categories are adapted from the Wholeness Wheel originally developed by the InterLutheran Coordinating Committee on Ministerial Health and Wellness, 1997, and used in Ministerial Health and Wellness 2002, ELCA Division for Ministry and Board of Pensions.

Chapter 6 Tool

Reviewing Ministry Goals and Achievements

On an annual basis, review the ministry goals established last year (or the priorities outlined on the Statement Form in the pastor's call documents) and discuss how the pastor, staff, and laity have contributed toward the meeting of each goal.

Provide each person participating in the evaluation process with a list of the ministry goals and a copy of this worksheet for each goal.

1. A ministry goal for this year was

2. I have attempted to carry out this goal by

3. I have seen the pastor, staff, or other members of the congregation carry out this goal by

4. Select the statement that best describes your current thoughts about this ministry goal:

_____We have completed this goal.

_____This goal needs more time and work.

_____This goal is no longer necessary.

_____This goal turned out to be unrealistic.

5. Additional comments you would like to make concerning this goal:

Chapter 6 Tool

Performance Evaluation

Use this tool to enable conversation about the ministry of pastor and people over the last year. Discuss the four basic ministry areas and the overall ratings and record what is well done, adequate, needs improvement, and/or items for further conversation. (This tool is available as a chart at www.augsburgfortress.org/CLS.)

1. Understanding of ministry

Pastor demonstrates a clear understanding of responsibilities in this area (ELCA Model Constitution C9.03):

- preaching

- administering the sacraments

Council members demonstrate a clear understanding of their responsibilities in this area (C12.04):

- stating the congregation's mission, conducting long-range planning, and evaluating the council's activities

- maintaining supportive relationships with the pastor and staff and assisting in annual evaluation of their ministries

- modeling a faithful lifestyle

The climate or culture of the congregation encourages members to use their gifts for ministry in the congregation and community.

2. Caring for the needs of the congregation

Pastor demonstrates a clear understanding of responsibilities in this area (C9.03 and C9.12):

- conducting worship

- providing pastoral care

- offering instruction and services for confirmation and marriage, visiting the sick, and conducting funerals

- supervising the congregation's schools and organizations

- installing council members and administering discipline with the council

- keeping accurate records on baptisms, confirmations, marriages, burials, communicants, and membership

- submitting statistics to the synod annually

Council members demonstrate a clear understanding of their responsibilities in this area (C12.04):

- seeking to involve all members of the congregation in congregational life

- overseeing the administration of the congregation

- arranging for pastoral services in the pastor's absence

- handling the congregation's financial and property matters

- preparing an annual budget

- ensuring that provisions of the constitution are carried out

- submitting a comprehensive report at the annual meeting

The climate or culture of the congregation encourages members to assume responsibilities and leadership roles and follow through on their commitments.

3. Taking Christ's mission into the world

Pastor demonstrates a clear understanding of responsibilities in this area (C9.03):

- speaking for poor and oppressed people, calling for justice, and proclaiming God's love for the world

- encouraging qualified individuals to consider ordained ministry

- distributing information about the ELCA and its ministry

- encouraging the congregation to support the synod and churchwide organization

Council members demonstrate a clear understanding of their responsibilities in this area (C12.04):

- encouraging partnership with the synod and ELCA and the use of ELCA resources

- inviting qualified individuals to consider ordained ministry

Members of the congregation are willing to actively invite others to worship and other ministry opportunities, serve non-members in the name of Christ, and carry out the work of Jesus Christ in the world today.

4. Mutual ministry

Pastor demonstrates a clear understanding of responsibilities in this area:

- supervising staff members

- communicating well with the council

- caring for our mutual life together in ways that create a positive climate

Council members demonstrate a clear understanding of their responsibilities in this area:

- communicating well with the pastor

- caring for our mutual life together in ways that create a positive climate

The climate or culture of the congregation encourages members to care for one another and for our mutual life together in ways that create a positive climate.

5. Overall ratings

Overall, the pastor is functioning effectively.

Overall, the congregation council is functioning effectively.

Overall, our congregation is functioning effectively.

Chapter 6 Tool

Developing Ministry Goals

1. As a group, consider these questions:

  • Are there goals from last year that need to be continued?

  • Are there current ministries that are effective, but need to be strengthened?

  • Is our outreach to the community as strong as it should be?

  • In what specific ways could we strengthen our witness to Christ by interacting with unchurched people in our area?

  • In what specific ways could we increase our support of the people who are already a part of our congregation?

  • Are we fully utilizing our gifts to support God's people throughout the world?

2. Individually, before the next meeting, list up to four goals you believe will strengthen the congregation's ministry during the coming year.

3. At the next meeting, work with your group to develop a set of realistic ministry goals. Once the goals have been agreed upon, go back to each one and decide how the pastor, staff, and laity will be expected to contribute to carrying out that particular ministry goal.

Chapter 7 Tool

Checklist for the Personnel Committee

For each of the following items, place a check mark in the blank if the responsibility is regularly carried out. Place an "N" in the blank if the responsibility needs attention.

___ 1. The committee has on hand a written assignment for its work from the congregation's constitution, to which it is accountable.

___ 2. The committee has read and discussed the relevant sections of the congregation's constitution, bylaws, and continuing resolutions (especially the chapters on Powers of the Congregation, the Pastor, and the Congregation Council) and has verified that it conforms to the *Model Constitution for Congregations of the ELCA.*

___ 3. Committee members all agree that the primary focus of their work will be fairness to the personnel of the congregation.

___4. The committee has interviewed the congregation's attorney and insurance agent, and understands the issues involved in liability.

___ 5. The committee has met with the mutual ministry committee and with the review committee; all members of these committees are clear about their responsibilities. In cases where committee memberships overlap, all members are clear about the need to separate these functions.

___ 6. The committee has jointly reviewed the Letter of Call for the pastor(s) with special attention to the sections on compensation, and on specific responsibilities if there are multiple pastors.

___ 7. The committee has jointly reviewed the most recent action(s) of the synod on clergy compensation.

___ 8. The pastor, based on counsel from independent tax advisors, annually submits a request for how overall compensation is distributed, including the amount designated as housing allowance.

___ 9. The committee annually submits comprehensive compensation recommendations for the pastor to the congregation council, and these recommendations are included in the budget as presented to the congregation.

___10. The committee has verified that all required payments on behalf of the pastor (such as pension and health benefits) are made in a timely way.

___11. The committee has reviewed sections of the Letter of Call that deal with time away from the congregation, and has, in consultation with the pastor, developed clarifying policies as needed.

___12. Clear written policies on continuing education (approval of plans, time allotted, and funding) are in place.

___13. A clear system for the reporting and payment of reimbursable expenses is in place in the congregation. There are established procedures for complaints by the pastor or staff if payments are not made in a timely way.

___14. There is a publicized procedure for making complaints if the pastor or a staff member is subjected to sexual harassment or other forms of mistreatment.

___15. There is a publicized process to be followed in the case of allegations of sexual abuse or other illegal actions by the pastor, staff members, or other people working on behalf of the congregation.

___16. The committee has audited the safety of the congregation's working environment, including interviews with the pastor and staff about problem areas. Changes, as needed, have been recommended to the congregation council.

___17. Personnel files have been created and maintained for every staff member, including job descriptions and a delineation of the scope of their authority.

___18. Every member of the committee and congregation council has at hand the name of the synodical bishop and contact information for the synod office.

Printed in the USA
CPSIA information can be obtained
at www.ICGtesting.com
CBHW081245240424
7424CB00022B/36

9 780806 646510